THE LIBRARY
ST. MARY'S COLLEGE OF MARYLAND
ST. MARY'S CITY, MARYLAND 20686

D1780544

TWAYNE'S WORLD AUTHORS SERIES
A Survey of the World's Literature

CUBA

Luis Dávila, Indiana University, Bloomington

EDITOR

Lino Novás Calvo

TWAS 598

Lino Novás Calvo

LINO NOVÁS CALVO

By RAYMOND D. SOUZA
University of Kansas

TWAYNE PUBLISHERS
A DIVISION OF G. K. HALL & CO., BOSTON

Copyright © 1981 by G. K. Hall & Co.

Published in 1981 by Twayne Publishers,
A Division of G. K. Hall & Co.
All Rights Reserved

Printed on permanent/durable acid-free paper and bound
in the United States of America

First Printing

Library of Congress Cataloging in Publication Data

Souza, Raymond D., 1936–
Lino Novás Calvo.

(Twayne's world authors series ; TWAS 598. Cuba)
Bibliography: p. 134–43
Includes index.
1. Novás Calvo, Lino, 1905– —Criticism and interpretation.
 I. Series: Twayne's world authors series ; TWAS 598.
 II. Series: Twayne's world authors series. Cuba.
PQ7389.N65Z88   863   81–1939
ISBN 0–8057–6440–2   AACR2

for Martha

Contents

About the Author
Preface
Chronology
1. Patterns of Change   15
2. Organizational Configurations: The Intruder
   and His Fate   30
3. The Diabolical Mind   45
4. The Splendid Years   60
5. Consolidation and Silence   81
6. The Revolutionary Period   96
   Notes and References   123
   Selected Bibliography   134
   Index   144

About the Author

Raymond D. Souza is Professor of Spanish at the University of Kansas where he served as Chairman of the Department of Spanish and Portuguese from 1968 to 1974. He received his B.A. (magna cum laude) from Drury College in 1958, and the M.A. (1960) and the Ph.D. (1964) from the University of Missouri.

He is the author of *Major Cuban Novelists: Innovation and Tradition*, University of Missouri Press, 1976, plus some twenty-five articles in scholarly journals such as *Boletín Bibliográfico Mexicano, Caribe, Hispania, The International Fiction Review, Journal of Inter-American Studies, Journal of Spanish Studies: 20th Century, Kentucky Romance Quarterly, Revista de Estudios Hispánicos, Romance Notes, Symposium,* and *Texto Crítico*.

Preface

Novás Calvo once described his first meeting with Ernest Hemingway and pointed out how the celebrated American writer reacted to him:

What attracted his attention was that neither my manner of expression nor appearance matched what he knew about me: that—like him—I had been a war correspondent, that—like him—I had written stories of struggles and death, that—like him—I had been in the middle of things. There could not be a greater contrast: he was large and strong, I small and frail; his voice was harsh and firm; mine, weak and soft; he was blunt and arrogant; I, cautious and meek. Another paradox; Hemingway seemed like his work; I didn't seem like mine.[1]

This series of contrasts is significant because it reveals Novás Calvo's self-image, but, more important, it demonstrates his extraordinary sensitivity to the demands of existence and his recognition of the fragility and vulnerability of human nature. The contradictions between appearance and accomplishment, between the outer and inner man, are apparent in his observations, and, in many respects, these concepts can be applied to his creative works. Many of his stories concern individuals who confront circumstances that exceed their capabilities. Novás Calvo's works chronicle the struggles of characters who attempt to overcome adversity, and his stories examine the extraordinary tactics the human mind adapts in its efforts to continue participating in the dynamic flow of existence. The contradiction between the man and his work that Hemingway found so fascinating in Novás Calvo is essentially a manifestation of the paradox between life and art. The two can be intimately related, but they frequently achieve an independence from one another that can deceive the unwary critic. The apparent contradiction is also a good example of how human imagination can transform aspects of experience into aesthetic creations.

Novás Calvo initiated his literary career in the 1920s, and his works span half a century of Cuban literature. He and Alejo Carpentier are mainly responsible for the formation of a modern tradition in Cuban prose fiction. The present study, the first book in English on Novás Calvo, combines a survey of his artistic career with the close analysis of individual stories. It has not been my intent to discuss every work by Novás Calvo in detail, but I have dealt with most of his stories. My research has uncovered several early stories such as "El flautista" [The Flutist], "Vida y muerte de Pablo Triste" [Life and Death of Pablo Triste], and "El bejuco" [The Vine] that have been unknown to critics and forgotten by Novás Calvo. This study is designed to give the reader an understanding of the scope and significance of Novás Calvo's writings. The stories selected for critical analysis were chosen because of their quality or particular significance to the genre or Novás Calvo's career. Two periods have been singled out for special attention—the years surrounding 1932 and 1942. Novás Calvo published three major stories in 1932 in a leading Spanish journal, the *Revista de Occidente*, and this achievement extended his influence throughout the Spanish-speaking world. *La luna nona y otros cuentos* [The Ninth Moon and Other Stories] appeared in Buenos Aires in 1942, and it is the most significant volume of short stories published up to that date by a Cuban writer. Novás Calvo passed through an interval of inactivity during the 1950s. However, stimulated by the Cuban Revolution, he began writing again after leaving Cuba in 1960, and a chapter is dedicated to the writings of this period.

Translations of cited materials are my own unless otherwise noted. Acceptable English versions of Novás Calvo's stories were used when available. The Spanish texts of quotations of relatively inaccessible passages have been placed in the footnotes. This includes, for example, stories published in the 1920s and 1930s that have not appeared in book form. I wish to acknowledge the support of the General Research Fund of the University of Kansas and to thank my colleagues, John Brushwood and Michael Doudoroff, for their advice in the preparation of this study. A special thanks is due Guillermo Cabrera Infante for his careful reading of the manuscript and his helpful suggestions. I am grateful also for the gracious cooperation of Novás Calvo's wife, Herminia del Portal.

RAYMOND D. SOUZA

University of Kansas

Chronology

1905	September 22: Born in Granas del Sor, Galicia, Spain. Son of Lorenzo Novás and María Calvo.
1912	Sent to Cuba by his mother to live with a maternal uncle. Lived in difficult economic circumstances and began working at a very early age.
1926	Spent eight months in New York City.
1928	First published work, the poem "El camarada" [Comrade], appeared in the *Revista de Avance* under the name Lino María de Calvo. Eight additional poems appeared in the same journal between 1928 and 1929.
1929	First venture in prose fiction, "Un hombre arruinado" [A Ruined Man], published in the *Revista de Avance*.
1930	The short story "El bejuco" [The Vine] awarded a fifth place prize in a literary contest conducted by the *Revista de la Habana*. Since that journal ceased publication, the story appeared in *Social* the following year. One-act play "El ahogao" [The Drowned Man] and the story "Vida y muerte de Pablo Triste" [The Life and Death of Pablo Triste] published in the *Revista de Avance* and *Social*.
1931	Corresponded with Sherwood Anderson. Left for Spain in June as a correspondent for *Orbe*. Stories published in the *Gaceta Literaria*, *Orbe*, and *Social*. Resided and travelled in Europe, mainly Spain, from 1931 to 1939. Worked as a journalist and war correspondent and published in several Spanish and Spanish-American journals and newspapers including *Ayuda*, *Diario de Madrid*, *Frente Rojo*, *Mundo Gráfico*, *Mundo Obrero*, *Repertorio Americano*, *El Sol*, and *La Voz*.
1932	Three major stories appeared in the *Revista de Occidente*, the Spanish journal edited by José Ortega y Gasset.
1933	*El negrero* [The Slave Trader], a novelized biography of Pedro Blanco de Trava. Appointed secretary of the literary section of the Ateneo of Madrid. Published an article on William Faulkner and Ernest Hemingway in the *Revista*

	de Occidente. Translations of William Faulkner's *Sanctuary* and works by Walter N. Burns, Robert Graves, Phillip Gosse, and Manuel Komroff published.
1934	Translations of Aldous Huxley's *Point Counter Point*, D. H. Lawrence's *Kangaroo*, and works by Honoré de Balzac and Peter B. Kyne.
1936	*Un experimento en el Barrio Chino* [An Experiment in the Red Light District]. September 5: Lectured on Maxim Gorky at the Ateneo of Madrid. Supported Republican cause during Spanish Civil War.
1937	Falsely accused by Carmona Nenclares of having written articles against the miners of Asturias during a meeting of writers and artists in Madrid. Spent a night imprisoned, fearful of possible execution, but released when charges not proven.
1939	Fled to France after the collapse of the Spanish Republic.
1940	Worked as an assistant editor and translator for *Ultra*, edited by Fernando Ortiz. August 2: Married Cuban poetess Herminia del Portal.
1942	*La luna nona y otros cuentos* [The Ninth Moon and Other Stories]. Awarded the Hernández Catá prize for the Short Story the first time it was offered—for "Un dedo encima" [Don't Lay a Finger on Him].
1943	November 29: Awarded degree in journalism by the National School of Journalism, Havana.
1944	June 19: Birth of daughter Himilce. September 15: Cuban Ministry of Education awarded him the National Prize for the Short Story for *La luna nona y otros cuentos*. *El negrero* appeared in French (*Le Négrier*. Genève: Editions du Rhône, 1944).
1945	*No sé quién soy* [I Don't Know Who I Am]. March 15: Varona Prize for Journalism.
1946	*Cayo Canas (Palm Key)*, *En los traspatios* [Between Neighbors].
1947	Began teaching as a professor of French at the Teachers' School of Havana, a position he held until 1960.
1950	September 25: Communications Certification for Radio awarded by the Communications Ministry, Havana.
1951	Temporarily lost teaching position after a change in government, but regained post after a hearing.

1952	Translated Ernest Hemingway's *The Old Man and the Sea* at the personal request of the author.
1955	January 15: Professional degree conferred in French by the Arts and Sciences Faculty of the University of Havana.
1959	*El otro cayo* [The Other Key].
1960	Sought political asylum in the Colombian Embassy in Havana, Cuba. After spending two months in that embassy, left for the United States. Resided in New York City and worked first for *Bohemia Libre* and then *Vanidades*.
1967	Joined the staff of the Department of Romance Languages of Syracuse University as a visiting professor of Spanish.
1970	*Maneras de contar* [Narrative Modes].
1974	Colloquium held at Syracuse University in honor of his retirement. Speakers included Enrique Anderson-Imbert, German Bleiberg, and Raymond D. Souza.
1975	Fall and Winter issues of *Symposium,* a journal devoted to the study of modern foreign languages, dedicated to his works under the special editorship of Myron Lichtblau and Jaime Ferrán.

CHAPTER 1

Patterns of Change

I *From Spain to Cuba*

NOVÁS Calvo's early years were ones of economic deprivation and adversity.[1] Born in Galicia, Spain, in 1905, he was sent to Cuba when he was seven to live with a maternal uncle. Economically, Novás Calvo's life in Cuba was not much better than that which he had experienced in Spain. He lived with a number of different families in his new country and there was little stability in his life. As a child and young man, he worked out of necessity at a number of jobs throughout the island, and the diverse positions he held provided firsthand knowledge of life among the working classes in the city, country, and at sea. During this period he acquired a fascination for the automobile and the sea, the former derived from his experience as a taxicab driver in Havana, and these became frequent settings for his creative works. The variety of positions he held as a young man gave him an intimate knowledge of the customs and mores of several social groups, and provided insights he incorporated into some of his works. Many of his writings focus on individuals who confront social and economic adversity and who are haunted by a vague sense of not belonging. The struggle for a feeling of permanence in a world of constant change is a characteristic of Novás Calvo's narrative art and a condition that has marked his existence during most of his life. However, it should be pointed out that his personal background served as a point of departure rather than as a goal of his creative work. An artist frequently writes about what he knows intimately, but he must be able to transform personal experience into an aesthetic expression for his reader if he is to be a writer of universal significance. While biographical details can be helpful in understanding the background and genesis of some of Novás Calvo's works, it should not be assumed that his personal life and artistic expression are one and the same.

Novás Calvo made a trip to New York in 1926, an excursion he would prefer to forget.[2] He evidently entered the United States while working on a small sailboat as a rum runner, and after an eight-month stay in New York City he returned to Havana "with more scratches than dollars."[3] The visit did provide practical experience with English, a skill he developed further and used in the translation of American and English works into Spanish. Despite the erratic nature of his life and education, Novás Calvo developed an avid intellectual curiosity and read widely. He was particularly interested in Maxim Gorky, Panait Istrai, and Joseph Conrad after returning to Cuba from the United States, and he soon found himself fully involved in Cuban intellectual circles.

II *The* Revista de Avance

Novás Calvo was working as a taxicab driver in 1927 when a new journal, the *Revista de Avance* (1927–1930), appeared. The radical orientation of the magazine attracted a great deal of attention, including that of Novás Calvo.[4] His fortune began to change the following year when a poem of his was published in the Cuban vanguardist journal under the name of Lino María de Calvo. Novás Calvo wrote in 1931 that "one day I sent them a proletarian poem, the first of this type that they published, and they gave me the happiest moment of my life."[5] Shortly after this, he met one of the editors of the *Revista de Avance*, Francisco Ichaso, who hired his taxi one evening. As a result of this chance meeting, Novás Calvo was given a position in one of the major bookstores in Havana, and he came in contact with the leading intellectuals and writers of the day, most of whom were directly or indirectly associated with the *Revista de Avance*. It was an exhilarating experience for Novás Calvo although he sometimes felt out of place in the unaccustomed intellectual environment:

We used to go to the meetings of the *Revista de Avance*, and they talked of the vanguardist writers of Europe and America, and I listened and kept quiet. At times, writers from Mexico and Peru and other countries came, on their way through. I felt out of place and that I could not join into talking about things I did not understand very well—me, a taxicab driver. Many thought I was the one who cleaned the offices and they did not pay any attention to me. Then we'd say good-bye in San Juan de Dios Park, and I used to go, at night, to El Yauco Café to talk with the Apristas and the Communists that got together there. They spoke badly of those who directed the journal. They said that they represented the bourgeoisie and that all the bourgeoisie was rotten. They even attacked me because I was a friend of theirs, in spite of my proletarian poems.[6]

The 1920s was an exciting time to be involved in literature in Cuba. Writers and intellectuals took pride in their openness toward innovative ventures, and felt they could exercise a positive influence by searching for new values in politics and art. There were manifestos and declarations, and a sense of camaraderie rarely achieved in intellectual circles. A receptive attitude toward foreign achievements also existed along with an insatiable curiosity about what was happening artistically throughout the world. Writers and intellectuals were anxious to break with the past, interested in experimentation and innovation, and optimistic about their chances for success. They undoubtedly overemphasized their own importance and minimized the difficulties of creating artistic works of permanent value. They sometimes seemed more concerned with shocking their public than with creating meritorious works, and many of their activities seem self-indulgent to us today. In comments about the *Revista de Avance*, Novás Calvo has pointed out its desire to break with the past, but he feels that it did not construct anything of permanent value.[7] The journal did, however, provide an excellent springboard for the introduction of young writers into the literary world, and served as an exciting forum for new ideas and concepts. The major contribution of the *Revista de Avance* was in the cultivation of attitudes and values that opened the way to new modes of expression, rather than in concrete achievements during its brief existence. The journal was of fundamental importance to writers such as Novás Calvo for it encouraged and sponsored creativity, and, in the final analysis, this was its most significant contribution to the writers and intellectuals of its generation.

III Early Writings (1928-1930)

Between April 15, 1928, and October 14, 1929, Novás Calvo published nine poems in the *Revista de Avance*. A close study of the poetic process of these works reveals a decided movement from an intellectual stance that emphasizes sociological concerns to one in which artistic considerations predominate.[8] At this stage in his career he was struggling with fundamental problems of artistic expression as he examined the relationships between politics and art. This has been a controversial issue in Spanish-American letters since its inception and it is a concern that continues to trouble the consciences of many writers. The *Revista de Avance* actively considered the implications of this issue by publishing a number of responses by writers and intellectuals to a set of questions dealing with the nature of art.[9] To a certain extent, the problems of artistic expression that the *Revista de Avance* dealt with parallel Novás Calvo's early development of his own creative expression. One recognizes in the poems he published in the *Revista de Avance* a movement toward a commitment to man in a philosophical rather than sociological sense. For example, in the first two poems Novás Calvo published, "El camarada" [Comrade] and "Proletario" [Proletarian], the speaker addresses individual members of the working class and laments their oppressed social condition.[10] It is interesting to note that in both poems the speaker feels separated from the symbolic figures he addresses by his recognition of their sorry state, an awareness they do not share. These poems are quite different from a later work, "Miedo" [Fear], which is free from concepts of class and deals with aspects of the human condition.[11] This work presents life as a tragic affair and man as a creature surrounded by a hostile world. The reaction to this circumstance is one of fear, and the speaker indicates that apprehension or dread permeates the happiest moments of life. These concerns were more fully developed and artistically expressed in later stories, for the motif of terror became one of the major preoccupations of many of his works. Novás Calvo also revealed in these early poems a preference for the use of the first person singular—a technique that became a hallmark of many of his stories.

Novás Calvo's first work of prose fiction, "Un hombre arruinado" [A Ruined Man], appeared in the November 15, 1929, issue of the *Revista de Avance*, and it is a transitional piece between poetry and prose. The work moves toward the creation of an emotional tone that conveys the psychological weariness and spiritual defeat of a failure, Don Ramón. There is no action in the story and it takes place within a sequence of time that spans a few minutes. By concentrating on the emotional intensity of a few moments in Don Ramón's life, the author creates a psychological portrait of a man whose materialism has isolated him from any meaningful human contact. The author moves from the particular, Don Ramón, to general observations that convey insights into human nature that are as timeless as man. This transition is achieved by blending two distinct sensations of time within the story's structure. On the one hand, we have a description of a few isolated moments in Don Ramón's life, but, on the other, the imagery used in creating Don Ramón and his surroundings suggests a longer period of time. A feeling of decay, a sense of defeat, and an aura of weariness are clearly present in the story. For example, Don Ramón is described as having "the great sloth of the pagan gods" who "await the offering of a vestal virgin on whom to avenge the offense of time."[12] "El hombre arruinado" is a compact piece of writing that depends on poetic imagery for its thematic concentration and on the juxtaposition of two time sequences within a short narration. A large reservoir of human experience is released within the intensity of a few moments in one man's life, and this technique is a literary perspective that came to be used extensively in the 1920s, particularly by Sherwood Anderson. At this point in his career Novás Calvo was well acquainted with the works of Sherwood Anderson, but his creative writings moved to a broader use of plot. The significance of "Un hombre arruinado" is that it marks an incorporation of poetical devices into prose fiction and Novás Calvo's realization that intuitive procedures could be used in a genre that had been greatly influenced by the demands of rationality.

"Un hombre arruinado" was followed in 1930 by the appearance of a one-act play in the *Revista de Avance* and a short story in *Social*.[13] Although both of these works are the products of a young writer, they do reveal the development of important elements in Novás Calvo's writings. The play, "El ahogao" [A Drowned Man], reproduces the language of the working class and is a forerunner of his imaginative use of popular language. In this work the author simply reproduces the speech of workers, but he later learned how to use popular language as a part of a creative process. That is, he discovered ways to embody poetic procedures into popular expression without the necessity of using the highly literary language of "Un hombre arruinado." The story "Vida y muerte de Pablo Triste" [The Life and Death of Pablo Triste] reflects an interest in plot development and continuity, and it marks his movement away from writings that concentrate on the creation of a single emotional tone within a restricted period of time. "Vida y muerte de Pablo Triste" also contains the initial use of a surprise ending which contradicts the reader's expectations and produces an ironic effect. This technique was further developed and refined in stories such as "La noche de Ramón Yendía" (1942) [The Dark Night of Ramón Yendía], "La visión de Tamaría" (1946) [The Vision of Tamaría], and "La vaca en la azotea" (1972) [The Cow on the Rooftop].

IV Toward an Authentic Voice: The Stories of 1931

Novás Calvo published four stories in 1931 and, in many respects, these works are indicative of the rapid development of his narrative skills. Three of the stories employ narration in the first person singular; "El flautista" [The Flutist] which was signed February 13, 1931, is the only story that used third-person narration. This particular work is short and highly impressionistic and deals with the mystery and fascinating attractiveness of death. The three characters that appear in "El flautista" belong to the same family, but they all remain nameless. This anonymity underscores the importance of the flute in the work, and as the story unfolds the reader begins to recognize that the musical instrument is the protagonist.

The older brother of the family is ill and dying, and his favorite pastime is playing a flute which has a haunting and fascinating sound. There are suggestions that the flute has a life of its own, as if the essence of its song were independent of the player. One of the devices that suggests the older brother's impending death is the symbolic use of the color white. He is described as if death's whiteness were slowly invading his being: "The whites of his eyes were each day whiter, and the white sheet that was encircling his inner life was becoming translucent through his skin. If life could continue after death, it would arrive one day when one's skin would be completely white from the contamination of death's whiteness."[14] The older brother dies and the survivors find themselves unable to resist playing the flute. The mother realizes that the musical instrument is mysteriously dominating their lives, but she is unable to resist its compelling attraction. She regards the flute as a transmitter of death and visualizes the musical instrument as converting its players into a flute, that is, as an extension of death. It is the instrument that renders the music, and the characters become notes in its melody of destruction.

Death is also an important element in "La cabeza pensante" [A Thinking Man] which appeared in May, 1931. In this work a taxicab driver narrates the story of Jacobo, a man who suffers from an "indescribable dread of life."[15] Unable to accept the harsh realities of his existence, Jacobo gradually becomes insane and seeks spiritual liberation by use of the occult. Psychologically twisted by events which are only vaguely suggested to the reader, Jacobo's flight from reality leads him to what he regards as an escape, his own death. Since the story is told from the viewpoint of a taxicab driver, its entire reality is confined to that individual's conception of events. One of the elements that is particularly significant in Novás Calvo's use of this narrative technique is the taxi driver's frequent incomprehension of his circumstance. The presentation of the events in the first person singular intensifies in the reader's mind the narrator's incomprehension, and this approach enhances the mystery the author is attempting to create. The narrator even begins his story by confessing his lack of understanding of Jacobo, a quality evidently shared by all who knew him: "Almost no one in the city knew Jacobo, during that time. He was different from other men, he was an odd man whom no one knew, whom no one remembered. What there was in him that people didn't remember, that didn't appeal to people's minds, I don't know."[16] That a man could be odd and still not attract attention heightens the unusualness of the situation and underscores a slight levity in the narrator's tone. These devices create distance between the narrator and the events of the story and focus the reader's attention on the incongruity of the situation.

The language of "La cabeza pensante" is primarily oral, and this gives the story a conversational quality that Novás Calvo also used in "Un encuentro singular" [A Singular Encounter] which appeared in the Spanish journal the *Gaceta Literaria* in September, 1931. In this story the protagonist, Carlos, returns to Spain from Cuba and goes back to a small village in Galicia to visit his mother after a separation of twenty years. Carlos cannot accept what he finds in his native village, and he decides to leave at night in order to avoid being seen. When Carlos describes his reactions to the village he states: "I continued feeling that my feet were sinking into my childhood, that my being was delving deeper into something that would manage to cover very soon my twenty years of internal struggle against the village."[17]

As the protagonist leaves the village, the only one who sees him is a gravedigger. In a sense, Carlos is attempting to bury his own past by denying it. Carlos runs away from what he discovers in the village, for after twenty years he belongs to another time and place, but the act is traumatic. The result of these contradictory feelings is a polarization of two emotional entities, of two selves, that enables the protagonist to relate his inner agony. After leaving the village,

Carlos meets a man on horseback, Rafael. They converse and the reader begins to realize that Rafael and Carlos are the same person. The inner tension created by Carlos's return results in a separation of the self into subjective and objective entities—one, Rafael, speaks the truth which the other, Carlos, finds difficult to admit or accept. This emotional disorientation, which in this story is associated with a lack of roots, is a motif that appears in many of Novás Calvo's stories.

Although "El bejuco" [The Vine] was the last story to appear in 1931, its composition most likely predates that of the other stories published in that year, particularly "El flautista" which was signed February 13 and "Un encuentro singular" which was published in Spain after the author's arrival in that country. The *Revista de la Habana* sponsored a literary contest in 1930 and "El bejuco" won a fifth place prize. Since the *Revista de la Habana* ceased publication before the award stories could be published, the work appeared the following year in *Social*. The contest was open to writers of all countries and the only restrictions were that the works should deal with a Cuban subject of the contemporary or future scene, and that the stories should not concern political or patriotic subjects.[18] The judges were José A. Fernández de Castro, Addison Durland, Gustavo Gutiérrez, Emilio Roig de Leuchsenring, and José Tallet. "El bejuco" is the most significant story Novás Calvo published before or during 1931 and it compares favorably with the generally recognized stories that appeared in 1932 in José Ortega y Gasset's prestigious *Revista de Occidente*. The rapid development of Novás Calvo's mastery of the short story is remarkable for it took place in a relatively short period of time between 1929 and 1931.

"El bejuco" is similar to "Un encuentro singular" and "La cabeza pensante" in its utilization of first-person narration and popular language. Like the protagonist of "Un encuentro singular," the narrator of "El bejuco" is directly involved in the development of the story and is not merely a witness of events. His view, however, is retrospective and as he looks back and recreates events, the past becomes an actual present for the reader. "El bejuco" begins and ends with the narration of a young man who tells of his strange association with Ramiro Montejo, a man in his late forties:

I was about twenty years old then, and for five years I had been travelling around the Island, working here, wandering there, always anxious to leave one job to begin another, and always with my pockets empty. I had never

Patterns of Change

had any great difficulties, however. My natural shyness—I can't say I've lost it yet—kept me away from risky adventures, and all my life had been a continual slow movement under the sun while my imagination brought me impossible gifts."[19]

The narrator takes up with Ramiro Montejo and his fortunes begin to change for the worse. Although it is the beginning of the sugar harvesting season, they are unable to find work. At Ramiro's suggestion they try to rob a store at a sugar mill, but the attempt fails and they are forced to flee. They run into the countryside and finally collapse in a sugarcane field. It is night and the moonlight and distant music of some blacks engaged in a ritual create an eerie scene: "The moon was rising overhead giving the cane field a golden hue. In the distance the drum of some living quarters could be felt where the blacks were celebrating some ritual. It was a solemn and gloomy beat. A funeral lament of living skins that was smothered in the suffocating calm of the night."[20]

The reference to the "living skins" of the drums is one of many descriptive terms used to suggest that telluric forces are at work. At one point the young narrator describes Ramiro as having "all the aspects that must have characterized the primitive inhabitants of Cuba."[21] And Ramiro himself speaks of the earth as being "vindictive."[22] These allusions to forces that emanate from the earth and that operate against men or possess them constitute a narrative theme Novás Calvo used in the stories of 1932, "La luna de los ñáñigos" [The Moon of the Ñáñigos], "En el cayo" [In the Key], and "Aquella noche salieron los muertos" [The Night the Dead Came Out to Haunt Us]. This approach was combined with his skillful use of language to create an aura of mystery and a sense of dread of the irrational forces that are operating in existence. It is a world not submissive to rational control, and its spontaneous vitality and uncontrolled energy constitute a constant threat.

Ramiro begins to talk as they are resting. After a period of silence, the distant drums begin to beat again and "on the horizon the dividing line between sky and earth had disappeared, and the stars merged in that total illusion."[23] All distinctions of space disappear as the night engulfs the men and this intensifies the isolation of Ramiro and the narrator and their importance to one another. Ramiro begins to speak of himself and his past, and his account has an intimate tone that incorporates his listener into a shared experience: "I was also born on this land, like you; and like you I fled from the home of my parents to be free."[24] However, much to the horror of his young listener, Ramiro's story becomes a gradual revelation of a compulsive need to kill that occasionally possesses him. He describes his incomprehension of the motivations that led him to strangle one man and the sensations he felt as his powerful hands did their grim work.

The young man's gradual realization that he is in grave danger parallels the increase in Ramiro's emotional intensity as the compulsion begins to seize him. In a very real sense, Ramiro warns his victim and this creates an ironic ambivalence in the relationship that is central to the experience created by the story. This relationship is intensified by the terrible fascination that Ramiro's story exercises over his listener's imagination and by the young man's need to escape: "That madness in the spectral calm of the country, was something that fascinated me. I felt it invade me, creep up my nerves, and curdle in my eyes. It was his breath, a dense foul smell, it was his skull-like face and his eyes, round, without eyelashes, that seized me. It was like a hypnotic force, not alive, but emanating from the putrid earth, as if the countryside were an immense cemetery and we were the only living beings."[25] The ambivalence in the relationship between Ramiro and the young narrator is paralleled by the use of two narrations in the first person. The skillful juxtaposition of the two first-person narrations and the duality formed by the young man's fascination with and fear of Ramiro contribute greatly to the story's success. These parallel or dual structures create dramatic tension which involves the reader in the work.

The young man finally overcomes the spell that Ramiro's presence weaves and he suddenly begins to run. Ramiro pursues him but he finally eludes his tormentor and escapes. Several days later he returns with other men to search for his would-be murderer, and they find Montejo dead at the edge of a stream. Ramiro had apparently fallen down an embankment while pursuing his intended victim. It is night when the men discover the body, but they can see because of the intensity of the moonlight which imparts a sense of irreality to the scene.

The story ends by concentrating on the murderer's hands which are described as being "like snakes" (p. 65). This image of the hands is particularly powerful for they are presented as visible extensions of some irrational force. Ramiro's body is described as an object and he no longer is referred to by his name, but simply as "the man." These references convey his loss of identity as an individual as he becomes an impersonalized manifestation of some nameless force that is felt and experienced but not understood. This depersonalization of Ramiro causes the story to end on a note of incomprehension and mystery. "The man was there at the edge of the stream. His fallen body, doubled over on top of itself, was now a shapeless mass. His head hung over the water, as if his last desire had been to look at himself in that mirror. Only his hands—those hands!— were stretching toward land, twisting like snakes for what could have been my throat—toward that which was the last object of his instinct: the stem of a vine."[26] The association of the hands with a vine conveys the irresistible and relentless force of the compulsion that drove Ramiro to kill, and completes a series of references to telluric forces.

"El bejuco" is the most satisfactory story that Novás Calvo published before 1932, and of all his early writings it is the most characteristic of the direction his future works took. Although submitted to a literary contest in 1930, "El bejuco" did not appear until December, 1931. Novás Calvo published "La luna de los ñáñigos," "En el cayo," and "Aquella noche salieron los muertos" in the *Revista de Occidente* in 1932, and these are the works that won him international recognition. Unfortunately, "El bejuco" has been a forgotten story and has languished unknown in the pages of *Social* for many years.[27] Unlike the *Revista de Avance*, the *Revista de la Habana*, or the *Gaceta Literaria* which were directed at literary and intellectual audiences, *Social* was a journal with a more popular orientation although it published a number of significant works by important authors. A Cuban critic, Ambrosio Fornet, has pointed out that "*Social* was not a literary journal but it would reflect, at times without intending to, all the high and low points of our cultural life between 1916 and 1930."[28] *Social's* overall importance in Cuban letters still remains to be assessed. The appearance of "El bejuco" in *Social* in 1931 is significant because it indicates that Novás Calvo's artistry had reached a mature stage prior to his publication in Spain.

"El bejuco" and "Un encuentro singular" are the most significant and rewarding stories that Novás Calvo published during his remarkably brief apprenticeship as a writer of short stories. The development of his artistry between the appearance of "Un hombre arruinado" in November, 1929 and "El bejuco" in December, 1931 is outstanding. "Un hombre arruinado" depends on poetic images, but the language is mainly intellectual and does not have the spontaneous quality of "La cabeza pensante," "Un encuentro singular," or "El bejuco." "Un hombre arruinado" also is atypical of Novás Calvo's stories in that it essentially creates one mood—a sense of failure—in its portrayal of one man and is devoid of plot. His next story, "Vida y muerte de Pablo Triste," marks the initial use of plot and reflects his dedication to storytelling. "El flautista" represents a more successful use of the creation of mood through descriptions of exterior reality, a technique also present in "Un hombre arruinado."

"La cabeza pensante," "Un encuentro singular," and "El bejuco" deal with emotional disorientation which results in withdrawal or flight. The central character of "La cabeza pensante" retreats into insanity when he cannot accept the harsh realities of his existence, the protagonist of "Un encuentro singular" flees his native village after a brief visit, and the narrator of "El bejuco" finds himself involved in a frantic escape to elude a murderer. One character slowly withdraws into madness, another's being is polarized into two entities, and the narrator of "El bejuco" is overwhelmed by fear and an instinctive desire to survive. These three characters respond to severe stress with extreme introversion, a split personality or physical flight, and they all confront irrational forces either within themselves or in the exterior world. Irrationality and the terror it provokes form a common thread in the three stories as the protagonists struggle to preserve their equilibrium in their confrontations with disintegrating forces. These works constitute early manifestations of Novás Calvo's interest in situations that create a primordial sense of dread.

Novás Calvo's predilection for first-person narration is equally evident in these works, and he combines this technique with the use of popular oral language. He does not, however, attempt to reproduce ordinary expression exactly. Novás Calvo uses popular language as part of a symbolic or creative process rather than as a static reproduction of reality. His language has a spontaneous and rhythmic quality and it is utilized as a springboard to stimulate the creativity of his narrators. Novás Calvo's narrators are weavers of tales and illusion and in his hands language frequently has a poetic and hypnotic force that captures the reader. Language is one of the most dynamic elements in his stories, and it operates as a vital force that draws the reader into the fabulous realm being created.

Novás Calvo uses a narrative procedure in "El bejuco" that incorporates the reader into the process of the story and heightens the work's dramatic tension. The first-person narration creates a personal quality, and the reader feels as if he were listening to one individual's story in an intimate setting. The narrator begins by relating a great number of details to explain how the situation developed and to convince the reader of the veracity of his tale. This same narrative approach, it should be pointed out, is used when Ramiro tells the story of his life. As the narration progresses, however, the peripheral details become less important and the narrator slowly moves us toward the apprehension of a single event or condition. We suddenly find ourselves in "El bejuco" in the country and as night approaches the distinctions between land and sky disappear. The distant beat of drums, which heightens an eerie premonition of the presence of elemental forces, ceases. One by one, the elements that link the characters to the reality that surrounds them fall away, and the only concrete entity is the presence of Ramiro's compulsion to kill. This process heightens the young narrator's feeling of vulnerability, and makes the presence of the irrational forces represented by Ramiro overwhelming. At this point in the narration Ramiro's madness seems to be the only thing that exists. In this narrative procedure Novás Calvo moves in on one element or condition and he slowly sheds peripheral factors. It is as if he were peeling a piece of fruit until nothing is left but the core, and in "El bejuco" the core is Ramiro's madness and his young listener's terror. These elements are synthesized in the image of Ramiro's restless and vine-like hands.

V *Correspondence with Sherwood Anderson*

During 1931 Novás Calvo corresponded with Sherwood Anderson. In one letter he expressed his admiration for Anderson's works and pointed out that he regarded the stories in *Winesburg, Ohio* as personal reminders of an essence he had left behind in Spain many years ago: "In my life as an emigrant, I keep these precious gifts as a consolation for that, forever lost, village life."[29] Novás Calvo also sent a brief poem dated January 10, 1931, that was dedicated to Sherwood Anderson. The poetic composition communicates the speaker's desire to live in a world that reflects human needs and creativity.

YO . .
Yo quiero un mundo
que se parezca a ti,
que se parezca a mí.
Yo quiero un mundo
asociado.
Un mundo de creación
que se parezca al hombre.
No quiero un mundo bueno:
No quiero un mundo malo.
Lo quiero,
simplemente
dolorosamente
    HUMANO.[30]

I . .
I desire a world
that resembles you
that resembles me.
I desire a world
linked.
A world of creation
that resembles man.
I do not want a good world:
I do not want an evil world.
I wish it
simply
painfully
    HUMAN.

    The poem is a plea that the world reflect human qualities or that it be an extension of the human condition; a positive view, perhaps, of the nature of man, or an indication of the speaker's awareness of contemporary man's estrangement from his own being. The allusions to alienation and creativity indicate the cause and hopeful solution to modern ills, and the speaker's wish that the world be an extension of human needs and desires. The speaker also intimately links creativity with unity and this parallels the affirmation of his individual identity and his interest in collective well-being. It is the individual affirmation, however, that stands out in the reader's mind, mainly because of the preponderance of verbs in the first person singular.

Novás Calvo also expressed his enthusiasm for the works of Eugene O'Neill in his letters to Sherwood Anderson and mentioned reading James Joyce. Regarding his reading preferences, he stated: "I am a one-eyed man in art, admiring the artists that feel like myself and ignoring the others. And I agree entirely with you: The art that has no irony, no life from the human heart, is not art."[31] He indicated his interest in the particular and emotional rather than the general and abstract, an inclination that has served him well throughout his artistic career. Despite the unpleasant nature of his visit to New York in 1926, his enthusiasm for American letters was not diminished, and his knowledge of English was sufficient to enable him to read Joyce, an undertaking that must have been a formidable task in the early 1930s. His letter to Sherwood Anderson reveals his interest in American literature, his intellectual curiosity, and his desire to become an accomplished writer.

VI *An Opportunity to Return to Spain*

In May and June, 1931 Novás Calvo published two humorous articles in *Orbe*, a weekly magazine founded by the prestigious Cuban newspaper, the *Diario de la Marina*. These articles consist of accounts of the day-to-day existence of drivers of taxicabs and delivery wagons in Havana.[32] They are presented in the first person singular, have a marked emphasis on humor, and integrate personal memories with imaginative explanations of different aspects of the trade. The director of *Orbe*, José Antonio Fernández de Castro, was impressed with these articles and he suggested to Novás Calvo that he go to Spain as a correspondent for the journal.[33] The offer was accepted and in June, Novás Calvo was on his way to Spain on the ship *Cristóbal Colón*.

CHAPTER 2

Organizational Configurations: The Intruder and His Fate

I The Return to Spain

NOVÁS Calvo arrived in La Coruña in July, 1931 and embarked on a career as a journalist and translator that provided a precarious existence for him during his eight years in Spain. On his arrival, he visited his mother whom he had not seen since his departure for Cuba some nineteen years earlier. When she asked him what he was doing and he told her he was a journalist, she replied that she was not surprised since he had always shown an inclination for work that did not require any effort.[1] Despite her unflattering comment, she must have felt that her decision years earlier to send her son to Cuba had produced favorable results. Within a month after landing at La Coruña, Novás Calvo was in Madrid, and in addition to the steady stream of journalistic articles he sent back to *Orbe*, he published a short story, two literary essays, an interview, and a review in the Spanish journal, the *Gaceta Literaria*.

From a literary point of view, Novás Calvo's first years in Spain were enormously successful. "La luna de los ñáñigos" [The Moon of the Ñáñigos] appeared in the January, 1932 issue of the *Revista de Occidente*, and this was followed by "En el cayo" [In the Key] and "Aquella noche salieron los muertos" [The Night the Dead Came Out to Haunt Us] in the May and December issues of the same journal. These stories brought Novás Calvo international recognition and mark his arrival as a mature and innovative writer. The distinguished Argentine critic, Enrique Anderson-Imbert, has described his reactions to these stories when they arrived in Buenos Aires: "I remember the astonishment that the first stories of Novás Calvo produced in me. I read them, in 1932, in the *Revista de Occidente*. . . I read them with amazement because they were unlike anyone else's."² The acceptance of "La luna de los ñáñigos" for publication caused Novás Calvo to begin thinking seriously of dedicating himself to the short story.³

II *"La luna de los ñáñigos"*

"La luna de los ñáñigos" continues the development of narrative techniques and procedures Novás Calvo used in previous stories such as "La cabeza pensante," "Un encuentro singular," and "El bejuco." "La luna de los ñáñigos" and "El bejuco" open with exclamatory statements made by a narrator who is attempting to catch his listener's attention with an abrupt and intriguing beginning. Both works center on individuals who are essentially outcasts and who upset the equilibrium of different social groups. This unsettling influence is manifested in "El bejuco" in the violence that a character randomly inflicts on others, but in "La luna de los ñáñigos" the outsider makes every attempt to be incorporated into a group that resists her presence. She struggles against a black community's superstitions and their belief that the white women in their midst are evil omens that have brought them misfortune and sorrow. Like "El bejuco," "La luna de los ñáñigos" deals with irrational forces and their manifestations in the exterior world and in the minds of the characters. Both stories use nocturnal settings, music, and moonlight to create an atmosphere that accentuates the dynamic nature of the story being presented.

Descriptions of exterior reality are used to create a mood and to convey the psychological state of the characters. The exterior world is deformed or is presented in such a manner that the apparent distortions either convey the way the characters perceive the world or their emotional condition. For example, drums that are used in secret rituals become a presence that communicates various things. In one instance, a character's inner stress is described by pointing out that "her waist had become tense like the skin of a drum."⁴ The same woman's introversion and withdrawal after the murder of her child is conveyed by references to the muffled sound of a drum: "All her senses had been locked up inside her in order to hold back the secret of the night and the moon, and since then the drum sounded differently, as if in its center there were a muffled moon, a rag moon."⁵ Percussion instruments are used throughout the story as symbols of the unrest and tension that permeate the lives of the characters. The reference to the "secret of the night and moon" is an indication of the animistic view of the world that permeates the work, an outlook that becomes more intense as the story unfolds. The association of the drum and moon, which appeals to the reader's senses of sight and sound, underscores the presence of unknown forces and the woman's relationship to them. Near the end of the story when uncontrollable fears are about to be unleashed in an orgy of persecution, the sound of the drums is associated with elemental and primitive forces. "The skins of the drums began to moan as if their voice were coming from a very distant jungle, as if it were nothing more than the very distant murmur of a jungle of wild beasts."[6] The individuals involved in the ritual are about to direct their fury against the imagined cause of their misfortunes for they feel they are engaged in a struggle against evil forces.

The moon is a pervasive symbol in "La luna de los ñáñigos" and its presence throughout the story conveys the mystery and fear that the unusual events of Garrida's story provoke in many of the characters. The narrator of Garrida's intrusion and incorporation into a black community is a white taxicab driver who knows most of the people involved. Although he participates in some minor episodes, he is mainly an indirect witness to the crucial events that are related to him by his black friend, Pombo. Pombo, a fellow taxicab driver, is a tough individual whom the other drivers respect and admire. When he suddenly begins to tell them of strange events in an agitated manner, he attracts considerable attention, although no one can understand what he means. The narrator comments on their incomprehension of what Pombo says and speculates that "it could be that its sense might be expressed in music, in the skin of a drum, on a moonlit night, if there were in our ears something with which to capture the meaning of the music."[7] The narrator's frequent use of words such as "if," "as if," and "might" convey his uncertainty to the reader. The narrator confesses his own inability to explain what happened and states: "I don't know why, but there was something in that story that refused to come out in words and that wanted to spill out all together and that welled up in one's eyes."[8]

Garrida, a foreign white woman, had married a black and lived with him in a black neighborhood. They have a light-skinned child whom a demented woman, Malvina, kills by burning. Malvina, it is explained, had gone insane after her daughter committed suicide by self-immolation. Garrida's husband abandons her after the tragic death of their child and she tries to acquire the speech, gestures, and dress of the blacks. When Garrida's husband reappears with another white woman, the black community can no longer tolerate the intrusions that they associate with bad luck and evil, and their wrath is directed against Garrida. One evening a group of participants in a secret ritual search for Garrida intending to drive out the cause of their ills.

The mad ravings of Malvina reveal her interpretation of the causes of her daughter's death, and her twisted and elemental reasoning provides a subplot that accentuates the main action of the story. "My daughter set herself on fire because she was black and because she had a white driven into her head. My daughter, Rita, was black like charcoal and the man she had in her head was white like light. Because of that my daughter turned against her skin and burned it. My daughter is now in the hell for blacks burning until a white arrives there who has to go there to give her his skin so that he can go up into the heaven for whites."[9]

Malvina's ravings reveal several important elements. Her version of her daughter's death includes Rita's contamination or possession by a negative presence, an attempt at sacrificial purification by fire, a condemnation to hell, and the hope of redemption through the intervention of an outside force. The use of the colors black and white is central to the symbolic process of all the action in "La luna de los ñáñigos." This chromatic dichotomy is indicative of contending forces and of an ominous conflict raging in the minds of the characters. The indication of Rita's guilt is also important for it contains a suggestion that she has become contaminated and can only be exorcised by sacrificial actions. The narrator associates Garrida's marriage to a black as motivated by a desire to rid herself of a sense of guilt for other transgressions. Rita and Garrida are possessed by guilt for actions that have somehow violated undefined limits. In many respects, "La luna de los ñáñigos" is a search for equilibrium and harmony by individuals and a community after their psychic sense of order has been violated. They feel threatened by chaotic forces that are undermining a natural order and they feel menaced by destruction.

The utilization of multiple narration is among the many devices that Novás Calvo employs to convey a feeling of impending chaos and dissolution; that is, as the story develops and tension grows, an increasing number of voices are incorporated into the story. Although it is impossible to arrive at an exact count because many anonymous speakers are used, there are well over twenty voices, and they tend to emerge in great numbers at tense or climatic moments. The reader is forced to cope with a gallery of voices, and he senses the formlessness that threatens to overwhelm individual characters and the community. In addition to communicating an impending sense of chaotic doom, this device enables the author to combine individual and collective views of events. Novás Calvo begins the story with the intimate account of a taxicab driver, moves to Malvina's madness and psychic dissolution, and then narrates the upheaval that Garrida's presence provokes in a community. Unlike "El bejuco," which focused on one essence and which was centripetàl in effect, "La luna de los ñáñigos"is centrifugal and continually expands until the tension becomes unbearable and an eruption of violence occurs.

Some of the blacks in the neighborhood decide to take action against Garrida, and they prepare themselves by participating in a secret ritual. Pombo explains the hypnotic effect that the movement and music of the ceremony had on the participants: "We only knew that the music kindled our blood and that our muscles moved of their own accord. The bonfire warmed us and softened our legs and our waists, and the drums roared like storms that shook us. No one saw anything but the fire and no one heard anything but the roar. We would have heard any noise that wasn't ours, of the blacks. No one heard it, however. No one heard or saw Garrida among us."[10] Garrida has so successfully adopted the gestures and movements of the blacks that they do not recognize her presence. When they go searching for her, they cannot find Garrida because she has become one of them. A policeman accidentally arrives at the scene and the search ends.[11] When the group realizes what has happened, its reaction is one of intense fear; the neighborhood is abandoned and becomes a "cemetery next to the sea."[12] The story closes on this ironic note and, in more than one respect, the group has become its own victim. Seeking to resolve a problem by collective action against an individual, they end up persecuting themselves.

Unlike Rita who committed suicide, Garrida overcomes her guilt and self-destructive impulses by focusing her life on being incorporated into the black community. In this respect, the story is a narration of her need for atonement and acceptance. Garrida is a foreigner and an outcast among both the whites and the blacks. The white Garrida moves toward the blacks seeking communion, and the blacks move toward her in search of vengeance, but the end result is an indistinguishable fusion of the two, for the duality they represent is overcome.

The presence of the moon throughout the story underlies its function as an intermediary between the contending forces symbolized by black and white. The insane Malvina sustains conversations with the moon and the persecution of Garrida occurs in the moonlight. As an intermediary between light and darkness, the moon is the focal point of a number of dualities including guilt and atonement, separation and communion, life and death, good and evil, chaos and order. These dichotomies, it should be pointed out, are dynamic and constantly shift with changes in point of view. Eventually, a synthesis of opposites is reached when Garrida overcomes the barriers that work against her incorporation into her elected community, and her success represents a revelation few can tolerate. When the participants in the ritual search for Garrida, they cannot find her for they are seeking an essence of which they form a part. Their pursuit of evil in the exterior world is condemned to failure, for the seeds of positive and negative forces are contained in all men. Because of this, all the characters in Novás Calvo's marvelous creation are children of the moon.

III *"En el cayo"*

A young man is chased by a compulsive murderer in "El bejuco," and in "La luna de los ñáñigos" a woman is the object of persecution and a spiritual hunt. Both works successfully convey an uneasy sense of torment as the characters are drawn into situations in which they are the object of unknown, irrational forces. This emotional tone, a feeling of being threatened or pursued by a menacing presence, is even more predominant in the next story that Novás Calvo published in the *Revista de Occidente*. "En el cayo" [In the Key] presents the agony and terror of a group of men who are overwhelmed and destroyed by powers they cannot control. Only two survive the unusual, grim events and one, a youth, attempts to sort out the various elements as he begins to narrate his tale. The boy tells of how he joined a group of workers on their way to a swamp where charcoal is produced. There are more than fifty workers in the group which is composed of different races and nationalities.

They begin the trip with a good deal of optimism, particularly on the part of the young narrator who looks forward to spending the money he will earn, but as the work crew moves closer to its destination, the atmosphere begins to change. They board a ship and the captain, whose father had been a slave trader, unconsciously uses gestures that echo the past: "His hand cut through the air in a zigzag fashion as if it were holding a whip. It's not that there was really a whip in it. All that had ended. But there was something invisible in all of that that the blacks secretly sensed, that spoke to them from the past."[13] As they travel, their surroundings begin to take on a sinister aspect: "The moon had dissolved into the sea, infecting it with a yellow pus, and the sea looked like a graveyard in the night. The moon spread eerie lights over the sea and we were like an ancient grave" (p. 242). This putrid atmosphere of decay, the reference to the "ancient grave," and the description of the captain who suggests the past are indications of the story's movement back in time. The vestiges of civilization slip away as the group penetrates the alien and foreboding area, and the men are slowly reduced to their most elemental being. When they arrive at their destination, their leaders put on uniforms and watch over them with attack dogs and firearms. They are surrounded by hordes of mosquitoes, threatened by crocodiles and snakes, and fall prey to illness and fever. They are the captives of a devouring reality and of the company they work for, and they perceive that they are slaves. Novás Calvo skillfully uses the blacks in the story as a vehicle to create a slave-like atmosphere, a condition which engulfs all of the workers. The blacks are an exotic and almost alien presence at the beginning but as the work progresses and they all suffer the same fate, differences disappear and everyone is the same. As the story unfolds, "En el cayo" becomes a study of men under unbearable stress. The narrator frequently refers to the imaginative faculty and how it operates in such a threatening atmosphere: "There were still many months to go before completing a year, and no one knew what day it was. The key destroys memory and imagination takes over the senses" (pp. 253–54). Since they have no memory, they are devoid of a past. They are like primitive men attempting to understand and control a world that inspires awe and terror. The workers feel that they are surrounded by an animistic reality and that the exterior world is inhabited by hostile spirits that are trying to destroy them. Encircled by primal forces of death and disintegration, they attempt to cope in a most basic fashion.

Novás Calvo uses a number of narrative devices to convey the men's attempts to control or escape from their hostile environment and to communicate their fear. Threatened by death, the workers become exceedingly sensitive to time, and they resort to music in their efforts to suspend time's flow. The narrator describes the process in a masterful sentence: "To immerse oneself in that music was to abandon exterior reality and live without time" (p. 244). The blackness of the night becomes a symbol of everything the men dread. They huddle around a fire to protect themselves from the darkness that encircles them, and the fire is described as burning the flesh of the night. The night is converted into a living entity intent on swallowing life. The approach of night is associated also with the loss of space, a technique employed in "El bejuco," and the disappearance of space is related to the dissolution of time:

Then came the bottomless night. It had no sides or bottom and it was nothing but an empty void in the world. There was no water or land, and not even the palm trees could be seen, and he who was next to the fire saw human events from within. They were events that took place in the imagination and could only be seen before and after they happened, while occurring. Everything was happening there and it was all devoured by the night. (p. 252)

Around the fire the notion of time disappears as the past, future, and present are synthesized by the hypnotic state produced by the flames. The disappearance of time is conveyed by a verbal sequence that states that human events are seen in the fire only before and after they happen, but this is immediately contradicted by the insertion of "while occurring" which emphasizes the present. A synthesis of the three dimensions of time is thereby conveyed, suggesting that the notion of timelessness or no time endures while the men are in this hypnotic state and their imaginations are unrestrained. They use their creativity in their efforts to blot out objective truth and to overcome their fear. This causes the men to feel that they are merging with nature and recapturing racial memories that have remained dormant since time began: "The earth gave itself to us like a hot body, with the fragrance of breasts, and in our ancestral memory silent forms returned and our nerves wrapped themselves around them. . . But next to the fire it was worse. There one is a drum and one's guts tense up like a drum and everything else becomes lava. Then came that of which one cannot speak. Then what happens is a cold knife that crosses the night. Then comes the owl's crying hiss" (p. 253).

Despite the valiant flights of fantasy, the workers cannot overcome a primordial sense of dread that lurks inside them. The taut skins of the drums convey their tense state, and the references to the "cold knife" and the "owl's crying hiss" imply the cause of their fear. The coldness of the knife and its association with the night contrast vividly with a number of references ("earth," "breasts," "fire," and "lava") that suggest light, warmth, and life. The owl is a nocturnal hunter and its hissing sound announces its menacing appearance. In this instance, the owl and the knife can be regarded as omens of death and the men huddled around the fire are its prey. Antonio Portuondo has pointed out that Novás Calvo evokes rather than describes emotions, and the imagery he uses in the above quotation forms a good example of how he achieves this end.[14] Although Novás Calvo uses popular language as a point of departure for his stories, his works are verbal creations of amazing complexity.

The nightmarish conditions in the swamp intensify and the men feel they will never escape. All sense of time is lost, and one of the workers, when asked how long they have been there, responds: "We have always been here" (p. 258). This is true, in a sense, for they have been reduced to an elemental state in which the instinct to survive prevails. During another session of dance and music around a fire, the blacks, who are more aware of changes in their physical surroundings, recognize that a hurricane is approaching. Possessed by uncontrollable fear of the impending storm, they begin to flee. The overseers, unaware of what is motivating the workers, think it is a rebellion and they respond violently to the manifestation. All are possessed by terror for different reasons, and an orgy of violence breaks out. Finally, death in the form of a revolving circle sweeps down and all perish except two, the narrator and his companion Louro.

The storm is referred to as "the great demon of the world," and it is stated that the "sorcerers' incantations were impotent against the great demon" (p. 265). In this regard, it is possible to interpret the story as a revelation of the inability of man's creations to protect him from death. Music and creative imagination become impotent shields in the face of death's destructive force. The characters in the story are relentlessly pursued by dynamic, destructive forces and nothing they do saves them from their macabre fate. Two survive by chance, and as the story ends, they are adrift in barrels. Despite this pessimistic ending, the story does not offer a deterministic view of existence. Most of the work is devoted to how the men react to their situation and what they choose to do, particularly as far as their creative faculties are concerned, in responding to the crisis.

The ending is fairly brief in comparison with the treatment of the peril the workers face, and this is indicative of Novás Calvo's interest in how his characters respond to a crisis, rather than the outcome. "En el cayo" is a tale narrated by a survivor who was a participant in and a direct witness to what transpired, and, more important, he is an indication that life continues and survives the forces of dissolution.

Novás Calvo used similar narrative techniques in "En el cayo" and "La luna de los ñáñigos." The most striking similarity is the combination of a first-person narration and a series of voices. There are more than twenty speakers in addition to the principal narrator in "En el cayo," and this mixture effectively captures an intimate and individual as well as a collective and general view of events. The dichotomies that separate blacks and whites in both works are largely negated—thereby suggesting that the elements that divide men are less important than their common destiny. While the events in both stories are unusual, the two works contain logical explanations of what happens. One critic has pointed out that in "La luna de los ñáñigos," "the reader is not required to believe and the supernatural lives only in the minds of the characters."[15] The human imagination with its capacity to create and distort is one of the most important elements in "La luna de los ñáñigos" and "En el cayo." However, it should be pointed out that although a predominant relationship exists between the psychic and the physical, there is also a corresponding movement between the physical and emotional worlds.

IV "Aquella noche salieron los muertos"

"Aquella noche salieron los muertos" [The Night the Dead Came Out to Haunt Us], the last major publication of 1932, has an exceptionally fine beginning that introduces several important elements of the work. Like "La luna de los ñáñigos" and "El bejuco," the story begins with an exclamatory statement and plunges into an oral style of narration:

That Captain Amiana! He'd been there for ten years. There were people in the world that took him for dead, people that had known him. Not the rest of us, who had no one who knew us, unknowns. Emigrants. Amiana had a two-masted boat way over there in Havana, when he started to haul emigrants as contraband to the States. Poles, Syrians, Russians, Czechs,

Germans, Armenians, Spaniards, Portuguese, a lot of Jews. From everywhere. Amiana charged them four hundred dollars each and then he threw them overboard. Just like that, overboard.[16]

The combination of long sentences interrupted by brief, staccato phrases captures the rhythm of oral speech and allows the narrator to emphasize certain points. The short statements ("that Captain Amiana," "emigrants," "from everywhere" "just like that, overboard") underscore Amiana's importance, his ruthlessness, and his indifferent exploitation of unknowns from several parts of the world. The distinction the narrator makes between Amiana's infamous recognition and the anonymity of the emigrants sets up a social dichotomy that exists throughout the story. The characters are divided into masters and slaves, and this division is overcome only when one who shares power turns on his fellow exploiters in a sacrificial act of destruction. The intimate quality of the oral narration is combined with the presentation of many facts and details, a procedure which is designed to lull the reader into accepting the incredible events of this modern parable of human existence.

The discovery and establishment of Amiana's island were seemingly a chance occurrence. An unusual and rare movement of air, one the narrator points out has never been repeated, moves Amiana's sailing ship to the island. The wind is presented metaphorically as if it were in the form of a bird, and the ship is carried on the bird's wings to the island. The arrival on land is unusual; no one is aware that the sea is being replaced by earth until the vessel is stuck in mud: "The ship steered straight for land and did not realize it was navigating on ground until the mud had put it into drydock" (p. 286). The sailboat acts like an independent entity and this suggests that unusual forces are in operation. The area is described as limitless and the sailors find it easy to become lost in such a vast region. There is hardly any distinction between land and sea and everything is flat. Again, the descriptions are couched in metaphorical terms: "Everything was the same, and there was nothing to head for. It was like opening paths in the sea. All of the thicket was very low, a little taller than Amiana, very thick and all the same. It wasn't a forest with highs and lows like a musical scale. It was a sea, one body of water floating like a turtle over another" (p. 286).

The lack of vertical distinctions, the merging of the sea and land, and the limitless nature of the area all suggest that this is a region of cosmic proportions and almost formless. The reference to the turtle is also suggestive since it combines the geometrical shape of a circle (the top of the shell) with a square (the bottom of the shell or the four legs). In this instance, the turtle can be regarded as symbolic of undifferentiated materialism. Everything is level because there is no distinction between high and low or superior and inferior. It is a primordial reality of indistinguishable entities. This is perhaps best suggested by the mud that holds the ship fast, for the mud can be regarded as a mixture of energy (water) and matter (earth). It is an elemental world of undifferenced components, a mixture of matter and energy, of spirituality (suggested by the metaphor of the bird's wings) and concentrated materialism (the turtle).

Amiana changes all of this, for he and his men become an organizing force or intrusion in this primordial reality. They found a city, a complex social order is introduced, and the area is completely transformed. The indistinguishable flatness that existed before is symbolically replaced by the most extreme social distinctions when slavery is introduced into the island. When the narrator arrived, a miniature society had been formed complete with buildings, cemeteries, and a social order that divided the inhabitants into masters and slaves. The newness of this society is underscored when the narrator in an explanation of how Amiana captures men by force and brings them to the island states: "That's the way the Island was populated. That's the way a nation and a civilization and a language were formed. At first they had to invent words" (p. 290). A society is established by coercion and force and it is so new that words have to be invented. The story of the foundation of Amiana's domain is like a mythological rendering of the foundation of a civilization which, in this case, turns out to be a perverse creation. Amiana is an all-powerful presence in the minds of the slaves and his being achieves mythological proportions: "Amiana's origin was unknown. He was a solitary oak, and he seemed to have arms by the dozens, and hundreds of large bloody eyes, with lead bullets for pupils" (p. 294). It is a vivid portrait of a sinister, spider-like being who weaves the unfortunate destinies of many men.

Amiana's regime depends on violence, slavery, and the relentless and severe punishment of all who challenge him. He makes a fatal mistake, however, when he brings a man, Moco, to the island to serve as a sort of high priest. Amiana plans to use Moco to help him control his subjects by superstition and to create the impression that Amiana is a divine being. Moco is so adept at his role that he acquires great power and influence. The narrator makes it clear that Moco does not believe what he preaches, and that he uses his imaginative powers for manipulative purposes, but Moco's involvement in religion becomes so intense that it begins to drive him insane. The narrator's role in the presentation of all of this is dual. On the one hand, he faithfully reports the beliefs and feelings of those who are victimized by this hellish world, but, on the other, he maintains enough distance from these emotions so that the motivations of the leaders are revealed and understood. This combination leaves the reader suspended between two worlds or narrative lines—a rational and cynical apprehension of reality and an intuitive and emotional acceptance of the nightmarish existence on the island. The result is a revelation of the paradoxical nature of existence which even eludes and victimizes those who are masters of manipulation and illusion.

Moco devises an elaborate plot to destroy Amiana and his henchmen. The plan involves the poisoning of one of Amiana's top officials, an elaborate funeral procession from which all slaves are prohibited, and the explosion of dynamite in the cemetery to destroy all who participate in the funeral. Moco leads the funeral procession, playing a violin, and in Pied Piper fashion leads Amiana and his followers to their deaths. At this point Moco seems to be completely obsessed with death. He perishes along with his victims, but his sacrificial act allows the survivors to escape the island and to flee from their macabre existence. The description of the explosion and the events immediately preceding it has an hallucinatory quality. This effect is produced in part by an emphasis on the sensorial. Sound is important until the moment the explosion occurs, and then it disappears and the macabre event is felt and seen but not heard.

Moco was standing erect in the center, against the sky and sea, and no one saw him any longer. He himself didn't see or hear his own music, the singing of the fuse that was on its way under the ground and was about to arrive and revive all the dead slaves. Ten years of dead slaves. Those of us who were alive could feel them dying, living in death. Then we saw them ascend. We didn't hear the explosion. Our eyes had merged with our hearing and all our senses awaited the departure of the ten-year accumulation of dead. No one knew it, they felt it. And the terror!

The dead arose that night in a panic and went up toward the moon with the clothes of the freemen at the burial. We saw them ascend. I saw Moco among them with his mute violin. . . . (p. 322)

Along with the fusion of the senses of hearing and sight, there is an implied merging of life and death suggested by the association of the dead slaves with the clothes of the freemen. This is reinforced by the narrator's statement that those who are alive "could feel them dying, living in death." The explosion propels the bodies into the air, but for those who witness the event it is more than an eruption, for the dead come alive. Those who had observed the death of their masters flee and abandon the island. As he leaves, the narrator's preoccupation with Moco is revealed by the sound of oars that seem to moan Moco's name. Amiana's intrusion into the primordial reality of the island and the lives of his slaves is destroyed, and the destruction is carried out by a spiritual leader who sacrifices himself along with those who had exploited other men. Amiana had disturbed the natural order that existed on the island prior to his arrival, but Moco's destructive rebellion restores equilibrium and harmony. The perverse force represented by Amiana is countered by Moco, and the result is their mutual destruction.

The three stories published in the *Revista de Occidente* share a similar structural device—an intruder upsets the balance of an order that existed prior to his arrival, there is a reaction, and the final result is the creation of a void. A community attempts to expel what it considers an evil presence in "La luna de los ñáñigos," but its aggression becomes self-destructive and the community is abandoned. "En el cayo" presents the intrusion of a group of men into a hostile environment and they are ultimately destroyed. And "Aquella noche salieron los muertos" presents man as an alien force that corrupts and distorts a natural order. As in the other stories, man is victimized by his own destructive tendencies as well as by other forces. In all three works, those who survive either flee or are driven from the area where the major events take place, and the location is left without a human presence. It is as if man as an individual or species were an alien presence, incapable of finding a secure place in the world.

The first-person narration in "Aquella noche salieron los muertos" is the principal narrative device. Although a few other speakers in addition to the narrator are quoted, the first-person account is not combined with the extensive gallery of voices that were used in "La luna de los ñáñigos" and "En el cayo." In this respect, "Aquella noche salieron los muertos" is closer to "El bejuco" as far as narrative technique is concerned, although "El bejuco" is not as ambitious a story. "Aquella noche salieron los muertos" is much more collective in its approach, and its mythic implications involve a greater extension of time. The island can be regarded as an image of the world and its destruction as a liberating and perhaps creative act. It is also interesting to note that the stories become progressively longer. "El bejuco" is approximately six thousand words in length, "La luna de los ñáñigos" close to seven thousand, "En el cayo" about ten thousand, and "Aquella noche salieron los muertos," the most ambitious, contains some eleven thousand words. "El bejuco" and the three stories that appeared in 1932 share the utilization of ceremonial ritual, the moon, and music in nocturnal settings to evoke a mood or intensify the dramatic development of events. These elements are used as symbolic correspondences and they often are linked to the characters' perception of the world. Whether they attempt to control themselves, others, or their surroundings, Novás Calvo's characters respond with patterns of behavior that are individual and universal.

CHAPTER 3

The Diabolical Mind

I *The Cuban Novel in 1933*

THERE are a number of direct and indirect references to slavery in "En el cayo" and "Aquella noche salieron los muertos," and these stories are indicative of the attention Novás Calvo devoted to this subject in 1932. His interest in slavery found major expression in that year in the composition of *El negrero* [The Slave Trader], a novelized biography of Pedro Blanco Fernández de Trava. This extensive book of approximately one hundred thousand words was written in Spain, dated October 23, 1933, by its author and was published by Espasa-Calpe in Madrid in 1933. Novás Calvo has explained that he wrote the book at the suggestion of the publishers who were interested in a book of adventure, an economic opportunity that he accepted and completed in two months.[1] *El negrero* is a result of Novás Calvo's fascination with three subjects: the sea, men who live outside of the law, and black culture. Novás Calvo was a friend of Fernando Ortiz Fernández (1881–1969), the outstanding Cuban intellectual and sociologist, who began to publish books about black culture in 1905. Ortiz was inspired in his studies by Sir James Frazer's *The Golden Bough*, and Novás Calvo has pointed out that Ortiz was a major influence on many young writers in Cuba.[2]

Two other important Cuban novels appeared in 1933: Alejo Carpentier's ¡*Écue-Yamba-Ó!* and Enrique Labrador Ruiz's *El laberinto de sí mismo*. Carpentier's and Novás Calvo's works share an interest in black culture, and both novels are based on careful documentation. The content of these two novels is so unusual that the authors must have felt a need to base their works on historic or sociological facts in order to convince the reader of the veracity of the subject matter. To a great extent, they were both dealing with the problem of making the unusual and marvelous believable to their readers in an extended work of prose fiction. Novás Calvo had technically resolved this problem in his short stories, but this was his first novel written for a publisher who obviously had a broad reading audience in mind. The two works tend to present events and characters from an exterior point of view, but they reveal a strong awareness of the emotional and psychological aspects of their characters. These works are important in the development of the Cuban novel for they mark the initial attempt to integrate the fantastic and real. Labrador Ruiz's novel is more experimental and delves more intimately into the minds and emotions of its characters, to the extent that the distinction between fantasy, memory, and reality is not always clear to the reader. This novel diminished the importance of plot and introduced the fragmentation of form that was to become an important characteristic in the experimental novel in Cuba and Spanish America in the 1960s. The novels published by Novás Calvo, Carpentier, and Labrador Ruiz in 1933 mark a significant period and turning point in the growth of the Cuban novel.[3]

II El negrero

El negrero is an unusual book, an interesting mixture of fact and fiction. Although the author uses the historical data of the slave trade and Pedro Blanco's life as the framework of the book, the work reveals an imaginative dimension that is rich and appealing. The author's movement between fact and fiction contributes greatly to the novel's dynamism and stimulates the reader's imagination. *El negrero* takes place approximately between 1794 and 1854 (the years of Pedro Blanco's life) and begins and ends in Spain. Most of Pedro's life was spent away from Spain, mainly in Africa and Cuba when he was not at sea. *El negrero* is divided into three major sections of varying lengths. The first part is very brief and deals with the initial fifteen years of Pedro's life. However, the author succeeds in presenting in this short section a concise introduction to Pedro's personality and presents themes and techniques that set the tone for the entire novel.

Pedro lives with his mother, Clara, and an older sister, Rosa. Clara raises the children alone and is estranged from her family for having married against their wishes. Her life is one of economic difficulties and she earns a living as a seamstress. They live in humble and disagreeable circumstances and when she leaves for work, Clara ties Pedro to his crib. Pedro's reactions to some of the aspects of his early years are summarized in a paragraph that conveys the present and suggests the future. The passage begins with a reference to Clara's family's rejection of her offspring:

> But that had nothing to do with Pedro, except that he was born poor and rejected, and passed many hours of the first year of his life lashed to a crib. It was also like being born on a small island. There was an empty lot behind the hovel with an alley on each side where the neighbors threw out garbage, innards and fish scales. Dozens of cats came there to eat and fight. At night they gathered on the roof and fell clasped together and screaming from the eaves. The first thing that Pedro did when he could was to hurl rocks at them. I believe it was his only diversion, because his life soon was a wandering introversion. But he was always very fond of cats. There were always three or four warring cats within him, biting and scratching one another and doing the same to him. Cats with nine lives, angry, stealthy, with a touch of the tiger in them.[4]

The portrayal of the house as an island bounded by trash and the description of the cats' struggles over garbage operate as a symbolic presentation of Pedro's future. When he becomes a slave trader, he discovers he must contend with many others for the possession and control of slaves. Just as the cats fight over choice pieces of flesh, the slave traders callously scramble for human cargo, and they are not above preying on each other's spoils. The slaves are nothing but objects that are used to nourish their voracious needs. In this regard, the slaves become the offal of human greed and plunder. Pedro operates from ships during the first part of his career, and then establishes a slave trading center on an island on the coast of Africa. Pedro's bases of operation are islands of human misery, and this image of isolation conforms well with Pedro's solitary and suspicious nature. The association of Pedro with cats is used as exterior and interior manifestations of his condition. The cats' struggles over viscera suggest the nature of Pedro's movement through the world, and the projection of their conflicts into Pedro's inner being conveys the tensions and compulsions that torment and drive him. The language that Novás Calvo uses in these descriptions is very physical in the original Spanish and powerfully communicates a synthesis of emotional and material reality. It is as if Pedro were corporally possessed by catlike characteristics and becomes an animal of prey. This association appears several times throughout the novel.

Pedro is a timid and imaginative child, curious, intelligent, and exceedingly tough despite his fearful nature. As he grows up, his mother is more concerned about him for she "thought that that child was half-crazy, since he avoided people, never answered questions directed at him and talked to himself" (p. 9). His imagination is easily stimulated, and on one occasion a priest's vivid descriptions of Hell create in Pedro's mind a surrealistic vision of the abyss: "Pedro saw Hell clearly in his imagination, but he could never see Heaven. That aroused in him a labyrinth of lights and shadows that made him tremble. Every night on going to bed, when he closed his eyes, he saw descend a torrent of lands, houses, trees and people; he saw unattached eyes, gaping mouths, feet with wings, an apocalypse" (pp. 10–11). Pedro's fantasy is further incited by talks with an old sailor who narrates tales of the sea based on his personal experiences: "All the events in his career had been affected by secret forces that dwelled under the wings of the wind, in the bulges of the waves or in the heads of the clouds. These beings revealed themselves in different ways. The old man had seen one night, while becalmed, a multitude of cats howling around a ship, with St. Elmo's fire in their eyes, while the sailors died of thirst and threw themselves into the water and the cats devoured them. Another time, a shower of wax butterflies had fallen and encased the sails" (p. 18). Pedro's imaginativeness is also actively expressed in tales he narrates to his sister Rosa—stories which often terrify her and cause her to cry from fear. He takes to drawing figures on the walls, doors, and floors of the house—creations of the mythology produced by his fertile mind, and the narrator points out that it is Pedro's wild fantasy that makes him a timid child since he has the tendency to exaggerate the importance of things and events. Pedro's creative abilities are so powerful that even his mother finds herself cringing at some of his tales.

Clara eventually marries a widower who is a fisherman, and Pedro soon finds himself going to sea with his stepfather and his sons. Shortly after this Rosa becomes pregnant at the age of fifteen, and it is discovered that Pedro is the father. He is forced to flee for his life when a mob pursues him intent on punishing him for incest. He succeeds in escaping by swimming out into a bay and sneaks aboard a ship at anchor. He is not discovered until the ship is at sea. He definitively abandons his home at the age of fourteen, never to return.

Pedro's life at sea begins inconspicuously and he works on a number of ships. One vessel he joins as a crew member had once been used as a slave ship, and a shipmate, Collum, tells Pedro that the vessel "continued being a slave ship, as its previous essence persisted, and any man who enlisted on that boat acquired at once the soul of a slave trader. Things stain each other, brother, he said; the captain is like his pipe, the captain's wife is like the captain, and we are all like the ship. Collum heard, moreover, the screams of the souls of the blacks who had died on that ship. Pedro had begun by then to struggle against his emotions" (p. 40). Pedro elects to ignore Collum's vision of reality and he adopts an indifferent attitude to all he sees. He has begun to be alienated from his own emotions and being, and he attempts to bury his own fantasies in frenzied activity and action. As a result, he becomes a completely hardened individual, unconcerned about what he observes and oblivious to human suffering.

Pedro's isolation from his own emotions is forcefully conveyed to the reader when Pedro is on a slave ship and he looks into the eyes of a dying slave and records no reaction:

The boatswains had still not finished taking out the dead. One of them came up through the hatchway dragging a woman with a last glimmer of life in her eyes; thinking her dead, the boatswain had stuck his hook in her side and was dragging her with him. The blood that was flowing was still warm and her eyes looked at Pedro before coagulating. Pedro saw her fall into the water, with the little that was on her body, and float a moment face down and sink from the tug of pincers that pulled her down below. (pp. 79–80)

The author has selected his words carefully in this passage. The boatswain's hook and the pincers that pull the woman below the sea offer a vivid visual scene of macabre events and awaken in the reader a primordial dread of being seized or devoured. All of the forces at work here are nameless. The victim and the boatswain are anonymous and the entity that tugs the victim below the waves is unidentified, although we immediately think of sharks and the devouring reality and disintegration they represent. The only person who is identified and whom the reader knows is Pedro, and he is unmoved even by the eyes of the woman that peer at him during her last instant of life.

A comparison of the above scene of the woman's death with Collum's vision of the spirits that inhabit a former slave ship offers a good example of the contrasting styles that Novás Calvo uses in *El negrero*. One narrates scenes of reality in an objective and impartial manner, and the other creates fabulous visions of existence. This effective and skillful blending of the fabulous and the real constitutes one of the novel's most admirable qualities. So much has been made of the historical basis of this novel (the author, for example, includes a bibliography and a list of important dates in the history of the slave trade) that it is easy to focus on the factual and pass over the imaginative. However, it is the author's ability to create an awareness of the incredible aspects of existence that makes *El negrero* a dynamic work.

Some scenes in *El negrero* are so macabre that they seem to be a nightmarish mixture of fantasy and reality. To some extent, the unusual subject matter and events of the book create this combination, but Novás Calvo's skillful use of language is the most important element in producing this effect. On one occasion the slaves below deck are suffering from a lack of water and food and their agony is conveyed by the persistent murmur that emanates from their quarters: "A dull sound emerged from the depths of the ship as if the voices had no way out, as if someone were talking behind a pane of glass (p. 78). In another episode a ship is struck by an epidemic and the cries of the sick and dying are infused with a tangible and visual quality: "The moans came up through the hatchways as from a hell. They were gaseous and luminous screams, as if they had passed through the bones of a cemetery" (p. 168). The Spanish word that Novás Calvo uses to describe the screams is "fatuos" and this refers to the spontaneously inflammable fumes of phosphorous and hydrogen that emanate from putrid flesh, particularly in a graveyard. This is why "the bones of a cemetery" are mentioned in the quotation for they complete the association of the metaphor. The screams become luminous and visual in a suggestive and powerful synthesis of the senses of sight and sound. This same technique is used in another instance when Pedro's vessel comes upon the hulk of a slave ship that had fallen prey to pirates:

One night they saw to leeward the outline of a ship, almost motionless, with the sails in shreds and infested, the sailors said, with St. Elmo's fire. The night was calm, but moonless. Pedro gave the order to steer toward the ship and it was immediately recognized that there was no life aboard. It was a pirated slave ship. The skeletons of the crew were hanging from the yardarms and the blacks had disappeared. Birds had eaten the flesh of the sailors, who were like the pits of fruits hanging from the branches of a tree. Gaseous and luminous fumes emerged from the skeletons. Sharks were still swarming around, hoping that someone would fall into the water. (p. 175)

Pedro's crew mistakenly regards the light they see as St. Elmo's fire, but it is actually being produced by the gases emanating from the rotting bodies hanging from the yardarms. The calmness of the night and the absence of the moon heightens the sensation produced by the strange illumination, and this gives the scene an hallucinatory quality. The disintegration and dissolution of death's destructive force are symbolized by the birds and the sharks that devour the dead. It is an infernal scene and Pedro's ship departs the area as quickly as it can.

After many years at sea, Pedro decides to establish a slave trading center on the African coast, and this proves to be a profitable though dangerous decision. Pedro's personal fortunes drastically change after he succeeds in overcoming the opposition of competitors and extends his influence over neighboring tribes that supply slaves. Pedro becomes a powerful and feared man, and he feels secure or arrogant enough to devise his own flag to mark his domain. The creation of a flag is indicative of the egocentric madness of the whole venture; and its colors, black and royal purple, suggest the power and death under Pedro's control. Pedro's world in Africa is one of mythological proportions, and he lives as if he were a sovereign during a primitive period of human history.

The marked introversion that had periodically threatened him during his life begins to intensify, and a tendency to withdraw and isolate himself increases. He is joined by his sister Rosa and his struggle to suppress his emotions intensifies. When Rosa dies he leaves Africa, spends a short time in Cuba, and finally returns to Spain accompanied by his children and the mummified body of Rosa. Pedro slowly sinks into madness and spends his last years insane and in the constant presence of a box shaped like a ship. Pedro's caretakers suspect the box contains a fortune and when he dies they break it open, only to discover Rosa's mummified body. Pedro dies with his eyes open and when his daughter arrives, she discovers that Pedro's and Rosa's bodies are seemingly staring at one another. Pedro's obsession with Rosa reveals her importance to him, for she is reminiscent of a time when tenderness and love existed and innocence was lost. Pedro spends most of his life suppressing his emotions and imagination, and he dedicates himself to cynical and exploitive reasoning. He is a man estranged from his own being, and his incestuous relationship with Rosa, which is physical at the beginning and emotional at the end of his life, is indicative of his longing for his own essence. For he is a fragmented man who never achieves an emotional sense of harmony and completeness. This is a profound personal tragedy that is extended into the exterior world and becomes part of a horrible mosaic of collective cruelty and injustice.

III El negrero *and Subsequent Cuban Novels*

The historical period covered by *El negrero*, the movement between the New World and other continents, and the use of historical fact as a point of departure for imaginative fiction recall subsequent Cuban novels, particularly Alejo Carpentier's *El siglo de las luces* (1962) [Explosion in a Cathedral] and Reynaldo Arena's *El mundo alucinante* (1969) [Hallucinations].[5] Both of these works follow the procedure used by Novás Calvo and employ foreign historical figures (Carpentier, the Frenchman Víctor Hugues, and Arenas, the Mexican Fray Servando Teresa de Mier) to anchor their novels to historical events. In addition, all of the works exhibit an appreciation and awareness of the unusual and fabulous elements in their respective stories. Reality is at once wondrous and terrible and all three authors create an hallucinatory vision of events.

The central characters of these works are formidable individuals of great strength and will, but they are slowly diminished by the flow of historic forces and time. Carpentier's Víctor Hugues becomes an empty shell of a man who clings to whatever vestiges of power lie within his grasp. He is a solitary and lonely figure abandoned by former friends and lovers. Arenas's Fray Servando finds himself at the end of his life still surrounded by hypocrisy, and he is no more disposed than he ever has been to accept the world on anything but his own terms. He is like a madman running through a maze of mirrors forever pursuing the image of a world that is never to be. Novás Calvo's Pedro Blanco retreats into the imaginative introversion that had threatened him all his life, and he spends his last years insane and in the constant presence of his sister's mummified body. This relationship parallels the emotionally incestuous atmosphere that envelops two of the protagonists at the end of Carpentier's novel. The main characters in the three novels operate within the same historical period, a time of dramatic change. They begin by participating in the rapid changes transpiring around them, but they become victims of the transitions they once championed or exploited. In many respects, they are obsessed with power and are spiritually annihilated by its destructive seeds. It is interesting that

The Diabolical Mind

idealistic fanaticism or dispassionate and exploitive cynicism produce similar results as far as the main characters' lives are concerned. Distortions of the spirit and the mind are very much present in all three works.

IV Novás Calvo's Life in Spain

Although Novás Calvo's literary successes during his first years in Spain were extensive, his financial situation did not improve. When he first arrived in Spain as a correspondent for *Orbe* he received a salary of ten dollars a week. This amount was later reduced to five dollars until the magazine ceased publication in March, 1933.[6] These were the years of the Great Depression, and its effects were being felt throughout the world in the personal lives of most individuals. To supplement his income Novás Calvo turned to translating, an interest he had begun to cultivate in Cuba, and he translated works such as William Faulkner's *Sanctuary* and Balzac's *Les petits bourgeois* for Espasa-Calpe of Madrid, and *Kangaroo* by D. H. Lawrence and *Point Counter Point* by Aldous Huxley for Sur of Buenos Aires. During this period he also visited Germany and France and published in the newspapers *El Sol, La Voz,* and the *Diario de Madrid*.[7] Novás Calvo has stated concerning this period of his life: "I lived very badly in Spain and Paris where I lived on translations," and after a moment's pause in which he was lost in thought, he added, "I lived miserably."[8] His journalistic activities during these years included an eleven-part series on the history of gangsterism in the United States that appeared in the weekly magazine *El Mundo Gráfico* between October, 1935 and January, 1936. Novás Calvo had revealed an interest in individuals who live outside the law and who transgress moral boundaries in works such as *El negrero,* and this concern found further expression in his next creative endeavor, which was published in 1936.

V Un experimento en el Barrio Chino

The approach used in *El negrero* of presenting events from an exterior point of view is also employed in *Un experimento en el Barrio Chino* (1936) [An Experiment in the Red Light District]. This novelette contains some sixteen thousand five hundred words and is divided into eight titled sections. All but one of these parts are narrated in the third person, and except for the occasional reporting of some character's thoughts, the presentation is external. There is a marked dependence on the visual in *Un experimento en el Barrio Chino*. For example, characters are frequently referred to by references to their general appearance rather than by their names, and many descriptions of settings reveal a special awareness of the relationship between the intensity of light and color. This sensorial awareness is heightened by poetic descriptions of sound. The narrative consists of a series of scenes that are presented without great elaboration; many events simply happen and are not explained. However, the reader is not left in the dark as to what is occurring, for the narrator gives all the essential details and background, but the comprehension of events often is acquired after they happen. There are also a number of rapid transitions in *Un experimento en el Barrio Chino* despite the work's length.

The novelette opens and closes at sea on the private yacht of a beautiful, wealthy, and thoroughly corrupt woman, Jacinta, who takes drugs and uses them in her manipulation of others. Her life is a restless movement from port to port in search of new adventures and experiences. Physical sensation seems to be the only reason for her existence since Jacinta is constantly seeking to dispel the boredom that underlies her life. Although only thirty-five, her appearance is characterized by "a premature inner decay."[9] She is extremely cruel and on one occasion is delighted to participate in setting a dog on fire. However, she is an attractive woman whose striking beauty is highlighted by her intensely green eyes, an appropriate color for an evil enchantress whose sensuality often leads to death.[10] She describes one of her favorite pastimes as approaching life like a chemist who mixes elements in experiments to see what will happen. Instead of chemical ingredients Jacinta uses people, often with tragic results. She states at one point that "everything by itself has the same value. They are only transformed when one shakes them. . . When someone mixes and stirs them up. That's the way life is."[11] She declares in another instance that "life is so monotonous and it slips away, it inexorably slips away. The seconds push against one another. In order to realize that you are alive, one has to create new situations. Isn't that so? Experiment with life."[12] Jacinta is accompanied by a motley collection of renegades and a blind guitarist who was abducted to satisfy one of her whims. The blind man never appears but his presence is felt through the sad and languid music that emanates from the lower cabin he occupies.

In the opening scene of *Un experimento en el Barrio Chino* Jacinta's yacht is sailing at night from Marseilles to Barcelona. The narrator comments that the occupants had escaped from an excursion into the centers of vice of the French city without serious consequences, and then directs his attention to a description of the boat as it moves through the water. One of the narrator's statements is suggestive of what is occurring on the yacht: "In the central cabin, the lights seemed to be fading from the erosion of a weak accumulation of energy."[13] The reader soon discovers that it is not only light, but life itself that is being extinguished. Some of the crew who are in an alcoholic stupor are described but not identified, and they are suddenly startled by the sound of gunshots. Their shocked reaction is followed by a description of the effects produced by moonlight on the water, and this intensifies the irreality of the scene: "A rising round moon had covered the sea with a spectral phosphorescence."[14] A staggering "black form" appears on deck followed by a "white figure" "without precise features, silent and vague." The white figure pursues the black form "like a sailboat towed by a tug," a description which heightens the contrast of colors and suggests the intensity of the interaction that is taking place.[15] A final shot is fired and the black form falls on the deck. Jacinta emerges from the shadows, and the reader begins to discover what is happening and learns that Jacinta has murdered someone she recently met. The body is thrown overboard and another of many sordid events comes to a close.

The author introduces the first part of this work by moving from an anonymous to a specified presentation of his characters. This technique accentuates the importance of the visual presentation of the scene and heightens dramatic tension by emphasizing the unknown. However, Novás Calvo does not use this procedure to introduce every section, for some are initiated by a detailed presentation of characters. He moves back and forth between these two techniques, and also alternates between denoting characters by their names or by distinguishing characteristics. On commenting on the technical aspects of this work, Novás Calvo has stated that "the style and technique are similar to those of a detective novel, presented in scenes, like cinematographic sequences."[16] This explains the rapid transitions and the presentations of some of the events. It is not, however, a definitive summary of all the techniques he uses. It is fair to say that Novás Calvo describes the predominant characteristics of *Un experimento en el Barrio Chino* when he points out techniques associated with the cinema and detective stories. These are important elements in occasional stories, but they are not distinguishing hallmarks of all his work.

Jacinta's arrival in Barcelona presents her with an opportunity to experiment with a young woman's life. A friend of Jacinta, Madame Catalina, is concerned about her daughter's relationship with a young man she considers an undesirable suitor and she asks for Jacinta's help. Jacinta arranges a dinner party on her yacht, introduces the woman's daughter, Casilda, to Rodea, one of the members of her crew, and plies her guest with drugs and alcohol. They then leave for the red light district of Barcelona in search of diversion and entertainment. Later in the evening Rodea takes Casilda to a hotel. Shortly after this, there is a great deal of activity in the street in front of the hotel as people are attracted by horrible screams; one of Jacinta's companions enters the hotel to see what has happened. He returns visibly upset, leaves a message that Madame Catalina be informed that her daughter has been involved in an accident, and then he and Jacinta leave for the yacht. As soon as they arrive, the mooring lines are cut and the boat makes a hasty departure.

At this point there is a change in scene and the reader discovers that the desk clerk at the hotel is speaking and explaining what took place. He begins by answering a question, which the reader assumes is part of an interrogation, and proceeds to narrate in an engaging and detailed fashion the customary routine of the hotel and how the strange couple that rented a room had attracted his attention. The clerk's narration is a skillful combination of important and extraneous details that makes this section the most successful part of *Un experimento en el Barrio Chino*. On one occasion, for example, the clerk explains how he was startled to be awakened from a nap, took his pulse, and concluded he had been dreaming. He reports all his thoughts as he carries on a dialogue with himself and states: "That's strange, I said to myself; I haven't dreamed in years, not since I got married."[17] He then goes upstairs, observes the couple through a peephole, and watches as Rodea attempts to seduce Casilda. A violent struggle ensues and she stabs him to death with a pair of scissors. The clerk concludes his story by stating that "she didn't stop screaming for an hour, until the police carried her off, still screaming. . . ."[18]

Casilda's mother is notified that something has happened, and she wanders through the streets searching for her daughter. The news of the scandal spreads rapidly; it is quickly surmised that

The Diabolical Mind

Jacinta is responsible for the tragedy and a group begins searching for her. A description of the area as dawn arrives matches the mood of the vengeful crowd: "The entire district was beginning to take on a livid color, purple and sepulchral."[19] The mob mistakenly takes Madame Catalina for Jacinta and pursues her in one of those tragic ironies so typical of Novás Calvo's fiction. Although she sustains some injuries, she does manage to escape and we last see her out of breath, confused, and bewildered by events she has scarcely begun to comprehend. This scene is juxtaposed with the last paragraph of the work which presents Jacinta on her yacht at sea. As *Un experimento en el Barrio Chino* closes, "Jacinta Sanromán was sitting, rigid and enigmatic, next to her lookout, with her lifeless stare lost on the horizon, toward the East. Her experiment had ended leaving only bitter dregs in the bottom of her soul, a desperate stagnation and depression, that would only be broken by the shock of a new adventure."[20] Jacinta's indifference and knowledge of events contrast markedly with Madame Catalina's bewilderment and grief. The location of the two figures at the end of the story underscores the ironic tragedy of the work and contrasts the results produced by foolish meddling and evil intent.

Jacinta is a curious figure characterized as being beautiful, malignant, and bored. She is somewhat reminiscent of the decadent heroines of some Modernist works, particularly the feminine figure in Julián del Casal's poem "Neurosis." Both women are employed as symbols of malignant and self-indulgent evil. *Un experimento en el Barrio Chino* and *El negrero* evidence a fasincation with evil, and in the two works human depravity is associated with emotional distortions and perversions of the spirit. We see in these works a preoccupation also present in stories such as "El bejuco" and "Aquella noche salieron los muertos," for all these creations concern individuals who transgress legal and moral boundaries. Except for Amiana of "Aquella noche salieron los muertos" who is destroyed by one of his own men, the protagonists are only punished or victimized by their own actions. They are prisoners of their own being and suffer some of the consequences produced by their emotional aberrations. However, they wreak havoc on those unfortunate enough to come in contact with them, and bad luck plays a part in the destinies of many characters who meet them. Life has a random and haphazard quality in the stories of Novás Calvo, and misfortune often lurks behind the guise of casual or chance meetings. However, once an event has been set in motion, it seems to glide inexorably toward a dramatic unfolding.

VI The Spanish Civil War

Novás Calvo was in the northern part of Spain when the Spanish Civil War broke out in July, 1936, and he managed to board the last train that arrived in Madrid from the northern provinces.[21] He supported the Republican cause during the conflict and remained in Spain until the Republic collapsed in 1939. The war did little to mitigate his concept of the irrationality of existence, and it intensified his appreciation of the uncertainties of human life. During a conference of intellectuals and writers held in Madrid in 1937, a man by the name of Carmona Nenclares accused Novás Calvo of having written articles against the miners of Asturias in 1934.[22] These were serious charges that could have resulted in the death penalty, and Novás Calvo spent the night incarcerated and very uncertain of his future. Many writers defended him, and the charges were dropped the next day since the accusor could not present any proof. Although he would have preferred to have left Spain at that time, Novás feared that his departure would confirm the charge. The irony of the entire event—the false accusation by a complete stranger, his near-execution, and his feeling that the charge made him an object of scrutiny—heightened his awareness of the illogical aspects of existence.

Novás Calvo published a sonnet in November 1936 dedicated to Federico García Lorca, the Spanish poet who was executed by a Falangist firing squad during the early months of the conflict.[23] The poem centers on a communication of the essence of the poet's art and the indignation that his tragic death produced. The complex syntax of the sonnet is reminiscent of some of the more abstract poetry Novás Calvo published in the *Revista de Avance* in the 1920s. A few months later he published a moving account of the funeral of a fallen comrade he attended in December 1936.[24] The pathos of the scene is vividly captured and contrasts with the nearby presence of militiamen who are practicing with new firearms. Although these were distressing events, they were only the beginning of the long nightmare of the war and his exposure to the carnage and social dissolution of a bitter civil conflict. Novás Calvo's experiences during the war were so intense that they have found little expression in his creative works. It was not until 1962 that a direct trace of this bitter part of his life appeared in two stories in which he used the names of Carmona and Nenclares to designate characters who represent blind forces of vengeance.[25] However, it should be noted that when Novás Calvo left Cuba in 1960, he left behind the manuscript of a book that contained three "short novels" that dealt with the Spanish Civil War.[26] The works were based on events he observed during the conflict and he had been reluctant to publish them because they were unflattering to the cause he supported. He perhaps best summed up his experiences in Spain when he stated that "what I saw in the Spanish war was enough to make me vomit for the rest of my life."[27] When the Republican cause reached its end in 1939, Novás Calvo was among the horde of humanity that managed to enter France. He arrived in that country practically destitute and was able to return to Cuba only after receiving funds from friends, particularly José María Chacón y Calvo. Novás Calvo once explained his debt to Chacón y Calvo by pointing out that the distinguished Cuban critic "was like a father to me, like a saint."[28] The years in Spain were over and for the second time in his life Novás Calvo found himself abandoning a cemetery of memories and experiences.

CHAPTER 4

The Splendid Years

I " 'Aliados' y 'Alemanes' "

THE differences between 1939 and 1940 in Novás Calvo's life offer a good example of how rapidly personal fortunes can change. After the end of the Spanish Civil War Novás Calvo found himself in France, and he had to depend on the generosity of friends to return to Cuba. The decade of the 1930s had been artistically fruitful and intellectually stimulating, but the events of the war and the precarious nature of his financial situation cast a pall over his achievements. In 1940 Novás Calvo was working for the magazine *Ultra* edited by Fernando Ortiz, a journal that consisted mainly of translations from the foreign press. Novás Calvo married the Cuban poetess Herminia del Portal in August of the same year, and in 1944 their only child Himilce was born. Two months after his marriage an excellent story, " 'Aliados' y 'Alemanes' " ['Allies' and 'Germans'], appeared in the Mexican journal *Romance*. These events marked the beginning of a fruitful and productive decade in Novás Calvo's artistic career and personal life. During the 1940s he published two major volumes of short stories, won literary prizes for his works, and initiated a teaching career. It was, in many respects, his most prolific and successful period. The only significant misfortune of the early 1940s was the death of an infant girl in 1942.

" 'Aliados' y 'Alemanes' " represents the culmination of the artistic skills and concerns that Novás Calvo developed during the 1930s. The story contains the exploration and review of origins of "Un encuentro singular" and is narrated in the first person singular like most of the works of the 1931-32 period. It includes settings and events that are reminiscent of the author's interest in slavery as seen in "Aquella noche salieron los muertos," "En el cayo," and *El negrero*. For example, the narrator of " 'Aliados' y 'Alemanes' " mentions that his mother had committed suicide by throwing herself into a boiling cauldron of sugar—a not uncommon act of desperation among slaves. It should be pointed out, however, that Novás Calvo does not use such references in this story to focus on a particular social institution of the past, but rather to create an atmosphere that reflects the warping effects of difficult socioeconomic conditions. The past extends its influence into the present through patterns of behavior and thought that were developed during a grim period of human history, and these negative presences operate as echoes of a past that has not completely died, but is on the verge of perishing. The economic dislocation created by technological change is one of the fundamental motivations of the events in " 'Aliados' y 'Alemanes.' " When the narrator attempts to convey the internal strife caused by his need to choose sides in the conflict, he refers to his contradictory emotions as cats that are fighting within him, a device also used in the characterization of Pedro Blanco in *El negrero*. Of all his previous works, " 'Aliados' y 'Alemanes' " most closely resembles "La luna de los ñáñigos" although there are a number of significant differences. The two stories share the presentation of major events in a shanty town dominated by superstition and hostile to the presence of individuals who are considered outsiders and evil. The social rejection and the psychological fear this situation creates are conveyed by the dichotomy between blacks and whites, and are manifested in the two stories by the appearance of a madwoman who haunts the neighborhood and is regarded as a threat to the lives of children. This setting functions as a background to the most important events, and the social group's prejudices operate as a foil in the dramatic unfolding of the stories. The neighborhood in both works is manipulated by a character bent on achieving his own ends.

" 'Aliados' y 'Alemanes' " takes place in Havana in 1915 and revolves around the conflict generated by the introduction of Ford motor cars into the taxi trade. Pedralves, who has a horsedrawn taxi, becomes the leader of those who try to resist the new technological wonder symbolized by the brash, devil-may-care Marcos Tilburí. The narrator is a child who lives with Pedralves, an older man who has raised the boy as his own ever since the mother committed suicide on a plantation. The story is a retrospective view of events, and the reader sees reality through the eyes of a child, although the passage of time permits the addition of details and knowledge that the narrator did not have at his disposal when the events took place. Although the narrator's family is involved in a defense of the status quo, he finds himself irresistibly attracted to the new machine: "A fight began inside me like that of enraged cats. One of the cats was what I felt for Pedralves and the other was my attraction to the tin lizzies. These had slid into my soul and in the end it would be useless to try to drive them out and remain loyal to Pedralves. I could not hate the Fords the way he did, and even Tilburí seemed to me haloed in a kind of nobility. I already adored him, because he was the man who knew how to drive the car, which was a god."[1]

The struggle between the two groups becomes bitter, and an enemy of Tilburí, Simón, takes advantage of the situation and tries to settle an old score by dynamiting Tilburí's car. Tilburí narrowly escapes death in the explosion and when he kills Simón in retaliation, Pedralves intervenes and publicly declares he is the murderer of Simón. Pedralves's sacrificial act is inspired by his love for the boy and the realization that his life is drawing to a close. His wife is dead, he is old and economically defeated by the cars, and he knows that Tilburí is the narrator's father. The boy was the product of a casual liaison on a plantation where Pedralves had worked as an overseer, and Tilburí had never known of his son's existence. The bitterness of the struggle between the two factions of taxicab drivers and the neighborhood's hatred of Pedralves provide logical explanations and willing testimony to support Pedralves's assertion that he is responsible for Simón's death. Pedralves's ruse succeeds with the additional help of false testimony by the child, and he is condemned to prison. Pedralves's sacrifice, however, enables the boy to begin living with his father and to embrace the future symbolized by the automobile. Pedralves finally bows to technological change and is a symbol, in his defeat, of moral generosity and sacrifice.

The success of " 'Aliados' y 'Alemanes' " depends to a great extent on the skillful presentation of two story lines that are interwoven into the fabric of the story—the economic struggle and the child's reunion with his father. This dual plot is paralleled by the fluctuation in the single narrator's point of view between events as seen by him as a child and reviewed by him as an adult. This binary structuring of plot and narrative point of view contributes to the story's dynamism and allows an occasional ironic observation to be made. At one point, for example, the narrator points out that Pedralves had once been an anarchist and states: "But he was no longer an anarchist. At least he did not think of destroying the established order, but rather of destroying the new order, the Fords which were ruining all the cabdrivers" (p. 247). This whimsical observation also reveals the essential choice the young narrator faces as he is torn between his loyalty to Pedralves and his willing acceptance of the new order manifested by the cars. In the final analysis, Pedralves's destructive tendencies are directed at himself rather than the exterior world, and he becomes a symbol in the story of an old order's willing sacrifice to insure the future represented by the child. The technological and economic conflict, in this regard, becomes humanized in a way the boy can scarcely understand.

The child's attraction to the Fords is characterized by a religious-like fervor. When he examines the parts of Tilburí's destroyed car, he explains: "For a time I lived among them, examining each broken piece, caressing it as though it were a relic. As though that were a shrine, a holy sepulcher, destroyed by the barbarians. Except that I adored the sepulcher of a god of the future, not a god of the past" (p. 251). The intensity of his emotions captures the ardor of an age that has enthusiastically embraced the machine and regards its exciting presence as a liberation from the drudgery of the past.

As the story closes, the narrator relates how his father came to pick him up and took him to live with him and his wife. After stating that he never returned to the old neighborhood or ever heard about Manuela the madwoman again, the boy tells of his joy at riding with his father in the driver's seat of a new car. The juxtaposition of these two statements is important for they indicate what he has left behind and what he has embraced. The negative aspects of the past which are conveyed by the superstitious neighborhood and the madwoman are abandoned, and the child rides into the future greatly exhilarated by the promise offered by the machine. The story closes with a reference to the two factions of taxicab drivers who had been referred to as "Allies" and "Germans" and the narrator explains: "That was how I left off being an 'Ally' and became a 'German.' But I did not know what was going on between the real Allies and Germans across the sea. Only much later . . . but what does that have to do with our 'Allies' and our 'Germans'?" (p. 256). It is left to the reader to answer the question that brings the story to a close, and if he so desires, he can think of the war as the first great manifestation of the destructive uses of machines. This ending intensifies the paradoxes conveyed by the binary structures that exist in " 'Aliados' y 'Alemanes' " for the oblique reference to World War I suggests that there are limits to the benefits of progress and the god represented by the machine. The subtle introduction of this possibility at the end of the story is characteristic of the artistic excellence of " 'Aliados' y 'Alemanes' " and of the complexities and ambiguities shrouded in the apparent simplicity of the narration.

II La luna nona y otros cuentos

Two singular events mark 1942 as one of the most significant years in Novás Calvo's literary career—the award of a prestigious prize in a national literary contest and the publication of his first volume of short stories. The Hernández Catá prize for the short story was first granted in 1942 and was named to honor the memory of the distinguished Cuban writer who perished in a plane accident in Rio de Janeiro in 1940. Novás Calvo gained the award for his masterful story "Un dedo encima" [Don't Lay a Finger on Him], a work that later appeared in *Cayo Canas* (1946) [Palm Key]. Novás Calvo's first collection of short stories *La luna nona y otros cuentos* [The Ninth Moon and Other Stories] contains eight works. Three of the stories that appear in this collection—"Aquella noche salieron los muertos," "En el cayo," and "En las afueras"—were first published in the *Revista de Occidente* in 1932, another fundamental year in Novás Calvo's career. "En las afueras" was originally entitled "La luna de los ñáñigos" when it was published in Spain.

In 1967 the Cuban critic Ambrosio Fornet described *La luna nona y otros cuentos* as "the most important book in our short story production."[2] Fornet stated in another essay that the short story in Cuba reached a mature form in the 1940s and Novás Calvo's achievements undoubtedly played a major role in his assessment.[3] The merits of *La luna nona y otros cuentos* were also recognized by reviewers who evaluated its worth soon after its publication. Andrés Iduarte declared in a review of the collection that Novás Calvo "has become, without any doubt, one of the best short story writers of the Spanish language."[4] And Hoffman R. Hays found Novás Calvo to be "a master of understatement and irony of situation . . . His artistry is particularly apparent in the subtle atmospheric tension which he creates as he builds his drama."[5] Hays's comments are particularly pertinent to "La noche de Ramón Yendía" [The Dark Night of Ramón Yendía], which is one of the author's most widely known and anthologized stories.

III *"La noche de Ramón Yendía"*

Novás Calvo has stated that he wrote "La noche de Ramón Yendía" in 1933 "under the influence of the political events that were taking place then in Havana. Those events impressed me to such an extent, that I abandoned any intent of 'creating literature,' in order to narrate a story simply and directly."[6] He had been somewhat puzzled by the story's success, perhaps because he did not submit it to the elaborate effort and meticulous care he usually devotes to his works.[7] Whatever the author's intent or manner of procedure may have been, the story's artistry and dramatic impact cannot be denied.

"La Noche de Ramón Yendía" is a story of existential anguish, of the anxiety and fear of a man who was forced to be an informer, and who fretfully awaits the appearance of men seeking vengeance. The story takes place in Havana on August 12, 1933, the day that the dictator Geraldo Machado abandoned power. When word spread of Machado's downfall, mobs took to the streets and participated in an orgy of violence and retribution.[8] Ramón is a taxicab driver whose car had been used by anti-Machado elements, but after being tortured by the government's secret police, he reluctantly agrees to be an informer. When the Machado government falls, Ramón's guilt convinces him that he will soon pay for his transgressions, but he vows to attempt to escape.

Ramón is a lonely figure who sustains himself and his family without the help of anyone. His existential anguish is portrayed in a memorable passage that enters Ramón's thoughts from the perspective of an omniscient narrator: "It seemed to Ramón that these were the last hours of his life, and that very soon, perhaps before daybreak, everything that his eyes could see and his ears could hear would have disappeared, dissolved into eternal nothingness as if nothing had ever existed in the world, as if he himself, Ramón Yendía, had never been born, as if all that he had loved, suffered, and enjoyed had never had any reality."[9] The emphasis on the sensorial and the emotional combined with the series of negations implied in the clauses that begin "as if " communicate Ramón's sense of aloneness and his awareness of the finite nature of his existence. Although the narrative point of view used in this story is not typical of most of Novás Calvo's stories, it is indicative of his versatility, and the technical approach is similar to that of another of his outstanding stories, "La visión de Tamaría" [The Vision of Tamaría] of *Cayo Canas* (1946).

Ramón's restless anxiety is captured by his aimless wanderings through the city in his leased taxicab, and as the turmoil and chaos he sees around him increase, so do his fear and panic. The breakdown in the social order parallels Ramón's gradual loss of his self-control, and these separate story lines converge in the work's dramatic and ironic ending. This binary presentation of narrative lines is developed throughout the story. Another important organizational device is the division of the story into two essential sections in which different emotional tones predominate. The first part concerns Ramón's efforts to dominate and control his own fear, and the second narrates a chase through the streets of Havana. The first section gradually increases tension until it becomes almost unbearable, and when Ramón finds himself being pursued, he enters into the action with a great sense of relief: "His bursting brain, which had been pulled in a thousand directions, tortured by a thousand wires, began to work lucidly and with a single purpose" (p. 157). The abrupt beginning of the chase marks the sudden change in tone, for Ramón's anxiety is replaced by purposeful action. In both sections physical movement is used to convey and qualify Ramón's emotional state. His fearful anxiety is embodied in the car's random travel through the streets, and this is replaced by the taxi's frenzied movement at great speed to elude its pursuers. The essential quality of Ramón's existence is defined by his movement through space, and when motion ceases, so does his life.

The chase becomes a long and tortuous affair as Ramón's vehicle is pursued by a number of cars. This infernal hunt presented from the viewpoint of the prey is the main structural device of the second part of the story, and one which helps explain the compelling attraction and popularity of "La noche de Ramón Yendía." As Ramón twists and turns his taxi through the labyrinthine streets of Havana, his frenzied movement becomes a dynamic symbol of his tortuous fear and guilt. Ramón's persecutors are convinced that they are pursuing one of the causes of their political ills, and their relentless chase reflects their intent to expel all of the demons from their midst. However, Ramón's frantic efforts to escape and his pursuers' desire to cleanse their society of political evil are frustrated by the story's ironic ending.

The chase turns out to be a mistake. Some of Ramón's hunters had thought they had seen a passenger hiding in his car, while

Ramón had thought that their actions had been directed against him. When Ramón's pursuers overtake his car and remove his bleeding body, they are amazed that no one else is in the car. No one recognizes Ramón, and they become convinced that he is an innocent victim of bizarre events. Their sense of guilt is not mitigated by the query of an old policeman who asks why they had killed one of their own, nor by a visit to Ramón's home that reveals his family lives in abject poverty. The only man who knew of Ramón's involvement with the government has been killed, so there are no witnesses to his transgressions. The final irony is that Ramón is alive when he is taken out of the taxi, but he is thought to be dead. As they attempt to unravel the truth of the situation, Ramón bleeds to death on a table. These multiple layers of irony intensify the ending of "La noche de Ramón Yendía" and leave all the participants in the chase in a state of utter frustration. Ramón's efforts to save his own life had failed, and his death had been caused in part by his own panic. His killers' attempts to seek vengeance result in their taking on the heavy guilt that Ramón had once carried, and their efforts to expel evil are thwarted. This dramatic ending is reminiscent of those in "La luna de los ñáñigos" and "En el cayo," in that violence becomes self-destructive and never achieves its intended objective. Ramón's pursuers are like the individuals who attempt to expel Garrida in "La luna de los ñáñigos." They engage in ritualistic hunts designed to cast out evil from their midst and they all fail. Garrida's tormentors become the victims of their own prejudices, and Ramón's murderers must carry their guilt for the rest of their lives. In the three stories intolerable tension disrupts a social order, and chaos and disintegration overwhelm stability. The disappearance of order is viewed in negative terms, and violent acts produce sterile results.

IV *"Un dedo encima"*

The hunt is also used as a structural device in "Un dedo encima" [Don't Lay a Finger on Him], the Hernández Catá prize story of 1942 which was published in *Cayo Canas* (1946). The hunt and the motif of persecution are elaborately developed in this striking story that differs from other works of this nature in that reality is filtered through the point of view of one of the pursuers rather than that of the victim or an indirect witness. The narrator, Mileto, is about twelve years old and is a member of a gang that becomes intrigued with Fillo, a youth of the same age as the narrator. Fillo, an outsider in the community, allows no one to approach him, and his presence has a somewhat unsettling influence in the neighborhood.

The process of Fillo's appearance in the story is particularly intriguing. First, the sound of his name is heard, then his presence is felt although he is not seen, and finally Fillo appears. The progression is from sound, to an awareness of his presence, to his actual appearance. This procedure intensifies the almost supernatural dimension that Fillo occupies in the mind of the narrator. For example, Fillo is seldom depicted as merely coming into view or going out of sight. He seems to appear out of nowhere or evaporate into thin air. On one occasion Mileto describes Fillo's movement as if he were "floating" instead of running, and this is only one of many such references. The dichotomy in the narrative fabric of "Un dedo encima" is related to basic attitudes or points of view. There is something magical in events such as the appearance and disappearance of Fillo for the narrator, but the text also offers logical explanations of these occurrences. The juxtaposition of these two views of reality gives the reader the impression that he senses that instinctive forces of great power are being unleashed, and that they can barely be grasped in rational terms.

The use of a young narrator in "Un dedo encima" is particularly effective for it creates the impression that Mileto barely understands what is happening or that his consciousness had hardly begun to emerge. Mileto and his companions seem to operate on a purely instinctive level, and the language of the story skillfully communicates this condition. The tone of Mileto's narration is fairly indifferent and evidences little sensitivity to the suffering of others. The impassive nature of Mileto's view of events is strikingly different from the fear and terror the hunt produces in its victim. This dispassionate tone is also vividly contrasted by the presentation of another voice in the story, the passionate and fervent declarations of Sabina, Fillo's mother, whose warnings and premonitions fall on deaf ears.

Sabina is an outsider in the ramshackle community she lives in, and she is scoffed at and mocked by her neighbors. She lives alone with a daughter, Limbania, who is having an affair with a young man. Sabina has not seen Fillo since he was a few months old for she abandoned him and allowed him to live with his father, a man of the sea who lived outside the law. When Fillo is brought to her after his father's death by hanging, she fears that the past will repeat itself and that Fillo will become like his father if he receives the same treatment the father did as a child. When Fillo becomes the object of the gang's obsessive complusion to capture him, Sabina admonishes the youths to leave him alone and predicts dire consequences if she is not heeded. The cycle begins its relentless turn and the community seems determined to spawn another emotionally twisted being.

"Un dedo encima" develops around three main concerns: Fillo, the community his mother lives in, and the gang's activities. The narrator devotes considerable attention to detailed explanations of his group's rock fights and conflicts with another youthful band, to the extent of discussing tactics. These games have a serious purpose and function as a preparation for grimmer business. One day they circle in on a cat and stone it, but their execution of the helpless animal is interrupted by a sudden cloudburst and the animal momentarily escapes. Fillo watches the circle of boys closing in on their prey, and he and the cat are closely associated in the mind of the narrator. Although we never see what finally happens to the cat, we do discover it is dead. In these games, the idea of death lurks in the mind of Mileto, and there is even an ambivalent association of the cat, Fillo, and death in his imagination:

Someone could have wanted to kill him like the cat, his brother. We were still aroused from our war; perhaps we were even thinking of killing Fillo without anything happening. He didn't have any family except Sabina—and she didn't count—and Limbania. No one would pay any attention to them. Limbania had a little voice like a skinny cat, muffled, and perhaps she might die from being so pale. Perhaps one could kill him, and bury him like the cat after the rains.[10]

This passage reveals the community's callous attitudes toward Sabina and her family and the intimate identification of Fillo, the cat, and death. The references to the demise of the animal and the speculation about Limbania's possible death intensify the reader's expectations that the story will have a violent ending. The narrator's ambivalence about the gang's intentions conveys the nature of his comprehension of events and his inability to understand their causes completely.

When the two bands cease their conflicts, Fillo becomes the main concern of Mileto's gang, and they decide to use lassos to capture him: "After the cat we thought about him, but without rocks. Now we wanted to catch him, to touch him, to grasp him" (p. 112). Mileto's band is motivated as much by curiosity as by a desire to purge the community of Fillo's presence. It is as if their efforts to capture him were really a frenzied attempt to apprehend reality. Since Fillo had seen the gang closing in on the cat and had observed the hanging of his father, the image of an enclosing circle has a special and terrible significance for him. Fillo senses that he is the object of some obscure and threatening process, and he decides he will not willingly enter the grim game.

The story's flow toward tragedy is suddenly reversed by an unexpected and bizarre event. The neighborhood eccentric, Apeles, a sinister figure who likes to bite people and whisper obscenities to young women, attacks Fillo and is stabbed for his efforts. Fillo vanishes never to be seen again, and Mileto seems scarcely aware that he or one of his gang could have experienced the same fate. When Fillo became the object of persecution, it is as if he had been chosen to be a sacrificial victim. Fillo refuses to participate in his assigned role and uses violence to break out of his circle of fear. Apeles operates in the story as a symbol of base impulses, and the act of biting Fillo can be regarded as a dangerous outburst of instinctive forces. In this regard, Apeles, who is nicknamed "El Químico" (The Chemist), functions as a negative extension of the forces that are motivating Mileto's band of ruffians. When Apeles bites Fillo he is described as if he were a dog, and this animalistic violation of Fillo's flesh is also a dangerous attack on his emotional being.

The description of Apeles's assault of Fillo is very precise, but it is combined with observations that open the event to broader considerations.

Prato saw him open his mouth slowly, and then suddenly, close it with that roar. He saw nothing more, in the meantime.

The rest must have occurred without time, outside of time. Prato didn't see it happen, but then the Chemist was there in the road, twisting around, screaming. And Fillo didn't exist. He never existed again for us. Then the Chemist got up slowly, with the knife stuck, sideways, in his neck.

That was all. We saw the Chemist again walking around, but no longer biting; and Fillo never again. We saw Sabina again washing tablecloths, and talking to herself, but we no longer would see or hear Limbania coughing, for a long time. And we would play at war again, but not with lassos.

"I told you!" Sabina said. (p.119)

This concluding section of "Un dedo encima" is typical of the language that Novás Calvo employs to combine the specific and vague and the realistic and imaginative. Apeles's attack is exactly presented, but no one sees Fillo's response, and Fillo's act is described as occurring "outside of time." Mileto then states that "Fillo didn't exist," but this categorical statement is then qualified by another that asserts "he never existed again for us." There is a great difference between these two negations of Fillo's existence, for one implies that he ceased to exist and the other that he was no longer present in the neighborhood. This stylistic blending of the specific and nonspecific creates an ambivalence in the narration that is intimately related to point of view. Mileto wavers in his presentation of events between the concrete and fabulous, and this offers a different way of expressing reality. We do not feel that we are merely witnessing the presentation of one individual, but a drama that is timeless in its implications.

We recall Sabina's voiced fears that her son will be like his father, that things will go on the same way over and over: "No, no, be careful! Don't touch him, I tell you. Take care! You don't know him. The same thing happened to his father when he was a child like him and because of that he had to flee and he became a pirate and bandit. He was always saying: You can talk to me, friend, but . . . don't lay a finger on me. He said it ever since he was a little child. Look I know what I'm talking about" (p. 110).

This quotation is indicative of the paradoxical nature of the story, for the sense of touch does not convey intimacy and human warmth, but fear and an almost pathological resistance to contamination. Sabina is not at all surprised by the turn of events, although Mileto and the reader are caught off guard. And herein lies the essential irony of "Un dedo encima" for the dramatic reversal of events is contrary to what all but Sabina expect. When Fillo stabs Apeles, he destroys and reverses the expectations of the ritualistic hunt. The ambivalence of the significance of these events and Mileto's narration intensify the paradoxical nature of "Un dedo encima," and this dilemma is heightened by the final words of the story, Sabina's admonition that she had warned everyone what would happen. This leaves the reader wondering which character or event most closely embodies the story's significance—the half-mad ravings of Sabina, the frenzied and terror-inspired act of violence of Fillo, or the cold and calculated hunt of Mileto.

It is interesting to note that Mileto is the most dispassionate character and voice in the story. His reactions seem to approximate most closely the mechanisms of primitive reasoning (or what the French anthroplogist Claude Lévi-Strauss terms the savage mind), particularly in his use of elemental logic. For example, since no one saw Fillo stab Apeles and the incident was being observed by Prato, it is concluded that the act took place outside the realm of normal reality. Mileto attempts to explain all events, and things that are not verifiable by the human senses must have some intelligible basis. This explains his imaginative interpretation of some occurrences and his efforts to organize what he perceives and experiences into a cohesive whole. Of course, Novás Calvo's artistic language embellishes this manner of thinking with an abstract and metaphorical expression.

There are indications at the story's conclusion that some things have changed in the community. Sabina and her daughter no longer are of much concern to the neighborhood and they are left in relative obscurity. Apeles stops biting people, and the gang returns to its wars, but never uses lassos again. Dangerous instinctive forces have been thwarted or frustrated, but Fillo disappears, evidently carrying with him his fear of social units. He is not incorporated into the community like Garrida of "La luna de los ñáñigos," nor is he physically destroyed like the taxicab driver of "La noche de Ramón Yendía." What becomes of his emotional and psychological being is open to speculation, but there is no doubt that it is decidedly negative. There is much in the characterization of Fillo that is similar to that of Pedro Blanco in *El negrero*. Both children are presented as being timid and imaginative. They are aloof and solitary and their gestures and actions are associated with the mannerisms of cats. They are taunted and abused by their peers, are finally driven from their communities, and resort to violence in dealing with a world that terrorizes them. Both their lives are associated with the sea, an area of great movement and restless disorientation in the works of Novás Calvo. "Un dedo encima" and *El negrero* are indicative of the author's concern with moral degeneracy and the internal and external factors that contribute to the dehumanization of individuals. These concerns are also dealt with in other stories of *La luna nona y otros cuentos* such as "Long Island" and "Hombre malo."

V "Hombre malo"

"Hombre malo" [A Bad Hombre] is the story of a man who is morally destroyed by his own sense of ethics and responsibility. The work uses a binary structuring of plot similar to that of " 'Aliados' y 'Alemanes' " and presents the account of Mario's moral transformation and the world of Havana taxicab drivers. Although Mario is a careful driver, he has the misfortune to run over a young girl who survives the accident but is badly scarred. Her unscrupulous mother, sensing that Mario is a very conscientious individual, invites him to live with her and makes it clear that the girl is his responsibility. The mother continues her promiscuous ways and successfully exploits Mario for several years until he undergoes a drastic change and becomes involved in criminal activities. He abandons the family and becomes a successful man, and his newly acquired callousness permits him to visit his former family without feeling a sense of responsibility for their care. The story is narrated in the first person by a driver who knew Mario and who devotes a great deal of attention to the taxi trade. His explanations of different aspects of the cab business are very humorous, and this part of the story is reminiscent of the journalistic article "Quemando gasolina" that Novás Calvo published in 1931.

One critic has expressed some uneasiness with what he regards as the moral pessimism of "Hombre malo." "The moral is evident: in order to survive in this corrupt society one has to become evil. The world then does not offer many possibilities of moral perfection."[11] In judging this comment, it is important to take into account the price Mario pays for his success. He becomes successful because he ceases to feel, and he therefore loses an essential part of his humanity. Mario becomes to a certain degree dehumanized like Pedro Blanco of *El negrero*. It is a mistake to confuse Novás Calvo's fascination with evil as a surrender of moral values. Rather, he probes the complex nature of man and some of the factors that lead to the creation of undesirable individuals. Novás Calvo's works are not designed to lull the reader into a comfortable view of reality, and they call our attention to human insensitivity and perversity. His stories chronicle the struggles of individuals to maintain their equilibrium in confrontations with a harsh and cruel world. Novás Calvo's works suggest that an admirable quality of the human spirit can be found in the individual's capacity to struggle against dreadful odds, and it is this unwillingness to bow to adversity that frequently allows his characters to transcend the tragedy of their personal defeats. At times when reality is too difficult to accept, characters attempt to blot out objective truth and embrace self-deception or illusion.

VI *"Long Island"*

There is certainly no moral ambivalence in "Long Island," a story that takes place on an auxiliary sailboat engaged in smuggling between Cuba and the United States. The narrator is a crewman whose responsibility is to care for the motor, but he has no idea as to what kind of goods they are smuggling. He provides a retrospective view of events and fluctuates between presenting the past as something remote and as an actual presence. His first introduction to the cargo is an unusual smell that jolts him: "I went on deck, to watch them set the sails and came out the two entrances to the compartments and the smell knocked me back. It was a distinct odor, that one doesn't find in perfume shops, nor in drugstores, or in clinics, or in morgues, but perhaps has a trace of all of them."[12] A suggestion of the exotic ("perfume shops") is blended with a progressive association of illness and death ("drugstores," "hospitals," and "morgues"). The narrator quickly discovers that on this voyage they are smuggling a group of French prostitutes into the United States.[13] Some of the women are addicted to drugs, and this fatal attraction parallels the fascination and repulsion the women inspire in the men. The crew members observe "these half-nude women, lying on the floorboards, smoking, and speaking that language that every sailor knows (because he had heard it in every parlor of every port of every country) and because of that, each time that he hears it, it awakens in him feelings of terror and repulsion as well as fascination of cold and dead erections (perhaps like those of hanged men)" (p. 119). The repetition of the word "every" conveys the monotonous sameness of the sexual ritual of love for sale and the mention of "cold and dead erections" vividly communicates the sterility and illusion of acts that arouse passion without offering emotional intimacy or warmth.

The boat has a difficult trip and at one point it is pursued by a Coast Guard vessel. Violent storms blow it off course, and there are powerful and poetic descriptions of the crew's struggles against the awesome forces of nature. When they are able to, the crew brings the women on deck and they are hosed down in scenes that recall the treatment of slaves in *El negrero*. The voyage is so difficult that some of the women perish and their bodies are thrown into the sea. The exhausted ship finally reaches Long Island, and the women are delighted when a black boy confirms that they are indeed on the island. The women and crew part company, and the narrator comments: "There was no moon, that night; there was no more light than that of the stars. In that light we had seen how the women went inland on the white road, toward their white illusion" (p. 139). The word "illusion" is used because although the women are on Long Island, it is not the Long Island of the United States. Instead they have been left on one of the Bahama Islands that bears the same name. This ironic ending and the hardships the prostitutes suffer during the voyage inspire sympathy in the reader. Although the women prey on the passions of others, and trade in deception and illusion, they are pictured as the real victims of delusion and exploitation. Although "Long Island" has not received much critical attention, it is one of Novás Calvo's most strikingly ironic stories and one of which he is personally fond.[14]

VII *"La primera lección"*

Novás Calvo stated in the preface of *Un experimento en el Barrio Chino* that he had once engaged in smuggling, and he undoubtedly draws from personal experience in creating many of his works. However, the importance of autobiographical elements in a writer's movement from personal experience to artistic expression can be overemphasized. "La primera lección" [The First Lesson] of *La luna nona y otros cuentos* offers a good example of how a skillful writer can transform autobiographical elements into a noteworthy literary creation.

"La primera lección" narrates a seven-year-old boy's departure from a small Galician village in Spain for Havana, Cuba. The child and his mother live with her family for she has been abandoned by the father of her child. Her family accords her little respect and she feels they are exploiting the boy by requiring him to work despite his age. She decides to send him to Cuba with a brother in a desperate attempt to resolve her problems and to provide a better future for her son. The pending departure of the child produces great consternation and conflict in the family and the atmosphere is charged with recriminations and resentment. It is a story of pathos and anguish born of the bitterness and confusion produced by irreconcilable emotional conflict. The one element that unites the characters is the poverty in which they live. The destitution they share allows for few personal errors or economic reversals for they have few resources on which to draw. The pathos of the story is created by focusing the conflict on the child who scarcely understands what is going on. He is an unwitting bone of contention among the adults with whom he lives and his reaction is to withdraw into himself. This defense mechanism is interpreted as an affront by different members of the family, including the mother, for they feel that the child has been prejudiced against them by others in the family. As the story closes, the child is finally leaving. He joins a group that is travelling together and the grandfather, who had taken him to this last rendezvous, is left behind.

It is tempting to point out and dwell on the autobiographical elements in this work, for Novás Calvo was born in Galicia, lived in circumstances similar to those in the story, and was sent to Cuba at the age of seven with an uncle. The absent father is also significant for Novás Calvo arrived in Cuba with an animosity toward his father that he would never lose.[15] A number of other minor details conform to Novás Calvo's personal past, and, in many respects, "La primera lección" contains more autobiographic aspects than any other story he has written. Although these elements are interesting and sometimes revealing, it would be a mistake to regard the story merely as an extension of autobiographical elements because it is primarily a literary creation and a work of art. An artist invariably draws material from human experience, sometimes personal and other times not, but in rendering these experiences into aesthetic form, he changes and transforms them. The adversities Novás Calvo faced helped shape his vision of the world, and this contributes to the tone created by many of his works. Life is a tragic affair for Novás Calvo, but his stories are not written to present this view. Rather, he focuses on how individuals cope with a harsh and cruel world and attempt to transcend their circumstances. These factors are present in "La primera lección," and it is important to consider the technical devices that Novás Calvo employs to transform his personal past and vision of the world into an aesthetic creation.

Although Novás Calvo has written stories that are narrated from a child's point of view, he does not use this procedure in "La primera lección." The narration is in the third person and is essentially objective and impartial. This is one of the many devices he uses to objectify the autobiographical elements in the story and to change the personal into aesthetic expression. The reader is allowed to draw his own conclusions about the characters and events, for the author presents details, descriptions, and conversations in a manner that permits the story to unfold in a natural and unobtrusive way. The characters mainly reveal themselves by what they say and do, and seldom by what the narrator says about them. The child's love for his mother, for example, is conveyed by his simple physical animation when she arrives from work. Her feelings are likewise revealed when she shares her portion of a meager meal with her hungry son. Evaluative words usually appear in the conversations as the characters reveal their emotions, attitudes, and values.

"La primera lección" opens with the description of a long and persistent rain, and this damp and humid setting contributes to the foreboding atmosphere of the story. A detailed description of the village conveys the poverty and misery of the area to the reader and he soon realizes that the dark specter of hunger haunts the imaginations of the characters. The pending departure of the child attracts considerable attention, and most people in the vicinity view it as an opportunity, although the immediate family's reactions are more varied. The child is the main focus of the story, but he remains nameless and never speaks. This lack of identity intensifies the child's apparent helplessness and gives his presence in the story an elusive and haunting quality.

The sense of impending loss that permeates the story is increased by the discovery that the grandfather's mare has been found dead. This represents a serious economic disaster for the family, and this tragedy parallels the pending loss of the grandson. At the end of the story the uncle who is taking his nephew to Cuba offers to replace the animal. This offer underscores the sorry plight of the family and the association of the child's departure with economic necessity. The harsh reality of brutal facts, however, does not mitigate the emotional upheaval that the child's trip represents.

When the mother admonishes her brother to give her son a proper moral upbringing, he replies: "As for your son not doing any harm to anyone, I have my own ideas. They only send good men from here . . . and fools. They cut off their nails and yank out their teeth; they castrate and tame them; and then they send them out to defend themselves among wolves. That's why I want to take this one off with me before he grows up."[16] It is a lesson that the child evidently is beginning to learn.

His reaction to the emotional turmoil is withdrawal. "For the first time he was showing himself to be timid, and with an irresistible desire to flee, to hide himself and avoid expressions of sentiment, genuine or contrived."[17] When the child leaves the house with his grandfather who is taking him to meet his uncle, an event takes place that indicates the boy is learning to survive. His grandfather had forgotten an umbrella and he sends his grandson back to retrieve it. When he arrives at the house, it is completely dark. He enters quietly and moves through the darkness without any difficulty. Although he hears his mother sobbing and practically brushes against her, he says nothing and avoids her and all the other members of the family in the house. His presence eventually startles an aunt who screams. He then grabs the umbrella and runs out without even offering an explanation or revealing who he his. His skillful movement through the darkness and his avoidance of human contact indicate his emotional estrangement, a necessary stratagem for survival. When he suddenly emerges from the darkness of the house, it is as if he has been reborn independent of the emotional needs of a young child. The first lesson has been learned, the price of survival in a world he did not create has begun to be met.

The grandfather leaves his grandson with a group of travellers that are to leave together. It is dawn and the company departs singing, followed by the forlorn child who is described as being lost. His despondent mood is intensified by the rain and contrasts with the optimism reflected by the singing and the appearance of a new day. Hope and despair form intricate parts of the same event. Most of the travellers are elated, the child is confused, and the reader is shocked by the enormity of the event that is taking place. This multiple perception of one incident contributes greatly to the success of "La primera lección." Novás Calvo's skillful use of this and other techniques enables him to objectify autobiographical elements and he succeeds in transforming the personal into an aesthetic creation. Among the narrative devices he uses to accomplish this are the creation of mood through descriptions of exterior reality, the use of impartial third-person narration, the avoidance of evaluative words, the utilization of a nameless and silent child as a central protagonist, and the incorporation of symbolic events.

VIII "*La luna nona*"

The general objective stance used by Novás Calvo in "La primera lección" is evident also in the title story of *La luna nona y otros cuentos*. "The Ninth Moon" creates an atmosphere of moral decadence and is similar in technique to *Un experimento en el Barrio Chino,* but it is developed within a Cuban rather than a Spanish setting. The story concerns the struggles between two half brothers for control of their dead father's farm, and a brooding expectation of violence permeates the work. Sensual passion and brutality lurk in the gestures and eyes of the characters, and stability and decency only form a fragile veneer in this world of elemental feelings and impulses. The spiritual decadence that was so prominent in *Un experimento en el Barrio Chino* forms a significant part of "La luna nona," and is most evident in the incestuous relationship that exists between one of the half brothers and his older daughter. The girl bears her father a child, and the young mother's inability to nourish the infant adequately symbolizes the spiritual poverty produced by negative patterns of behavior that are perpetuated from generation to generation. The explosive joy of a Chinese festival provides an effective counterpoint to the story's grim development.

The author creates an extremely visual reality. Attitudes and emotions are conveyed by gestures and physical mannerisms and positions. Sound and silence also play an important role in his portrayal of the seething passions of "The Ninth Moon." At the end of the story an ambulance appears, too late to be of any help, and as it approaches, its "white and ghostly form" is described as if it were gliding without sound over the road.[18] The scene has a spectral quality which seems to suggest that the ambulance is powerless in this small, decadent world of primitive emotions.

Novás Calvo attempted to re-create literally the language of the characters that appear in "La luna nona," including the halting, grammatically incorrect speech of individuals of Chinese-Cuban background. Although this type of discourse tends to intensify the elemental atmosphere, the oral language that appears in this story does not have the creative force it exercises in other works. In this regard "La luna nona" does not follow the patterns of Novás Calvo's most original and successful stories, and although it is a fine work, it does not compare favorably with the other stories in *La luna nona y otros cuentos*. It is significant that "La luna nona" and the earlier *Un experimento en el Barrio Chino* reveal an intimate knowledge of the writings of William Faulkner, an influence that tends to impair rather than enhance these particular works by Novás Calvo.[19]

The importance of *La luna nona y otros cuentos* was immediately recognized, and in 1944 the Cuban Ministry of Education awarded Novás Calvo the national prize for the short story for this significant volume. Ambrosio Fornet's statement that this work forms the most important collection in the development of the Cuban short story is no exaggeration.[20] *La luna nona y otros cuentos* marks the arrival in Cuba of the short story as a mature and vital form, and the volume represents the culmination of Novás Calvo's development of his artistic skills. These stories are uniquely Cuban, but universal works of art. They are as intimately linked to Cubans as their daily speech, but they move from the particular to the expression of general concerns, propelled by language of universal creative force. It is his skill at fusing the individual and universal that most indelibly characterizes the artistic significance of Novás Calvo's works.

CHAPTER 5

Consolidation and Silence

I En los traspatios

THE quality and productivity that distinguished Novás Calvo's literary output during the first years of the 1940s continued into the middle of the decade with the publication of *No sé quién soy* [*I Don't Know Who I Am*] in 1945, and *En los traspatios* [*Between Neighbors*] and *Cayo Canas* [*Palm Key*] in 1946.[1] Although it did not appear until 1946, *En los traspatios* is dated 1943 by the author. In many respects, this work represents a more effective development of some of the techniques and narrative procedures used in "La luna nona." Although not as extensive as Novás Calvo's most ambitious works, *En los traspatios* consists of over nine thousand words.

The first paragraph of *En los traspatios* is very brief; although this introduction contains only six sentences, there are three shifts of perspective in the paragraph. This technique is utilized in varying degrees throughout the story, but it is most pronounced at the beginning and end of the work. Reality is either presented as different characters see it, or from an objective stance that focuses on distinguishing details or images. The use of conversation is limited. The narration also enters the thoughts of selected characters so there is a decided alternation in the portrayal of reality from exterior and interior points of view.

The atmosphere created is similar to that of "La luna nona" although it is not quite as sinister. A family on the verge of economic collapse must contend with an emotionally disturbed child, a neighbor who is encroaching on their land, and a rebellious and willful daughter. When the head of the household, Cobos, discovers his stepdaughter is pregnant by the neighbor who is stealing his land, his patience and timidity reach their limits. Shortly after this discovery Cobos sees a form moving through the darkness near his home, and he rushes toward the shape with a machete in his hand. Unfortunately, the black outline is not the hated neighbor but his emotionally ill son. As Cobos pursues the form he suddenly finds himself falling forward and in a few moments his body becomes limp. The scene abruptly shifts to Cobos's wife and stepdaugher who hear a shot, and they discover the terrorized child had fired at and killed Cobos. Both the child and Cobos had seen black outlines and each had reached a hasty conclusion as to what it was they saw. They viewed what they carried in their minds, what their emotional states projected or exteriorized, and their distortions of reality produce tragedy.

The death of Cobos surprises the reader with its sudden although not unexpected impact. The quick shift in scenes and the impartial and objective narration of the physical reactions of Cobos's body cause the reader to react as Cobos does, with a feeling of incomprehension. First the event takes place and is not fully understood, a confused reaction occurs, and then final comprehension of events is acquired. The narration moves from this presentation of Cobos's death to an omniscient view that explains and interprets events, an admission, to a certain extent, of the limitations of the technique used in the presentation of Cobos's demise. Some critics refer to this type of narration as cinematographic, an acceptable term when it is applied to specific scenes and not to the entire content of Novás Calvo's stories.[2] The effectiveness of this device is limited by the reader's ability to visualize the scenes that are being presented, and by the author's skill at providing additional details or an explanation of events by other methods when they are needed. *En los traspatios* represents the most effective and artistic handling of this technique by Novás Calvo.

II No sé quién soy

No sé quién soy [I Don't Know Who I Am] was published in Mexico in 1945 and was dated 1944 by the author. This work contains approximately twelve thousand words, placing it as far as length is concerned in the same category as stories such as "Aquella noche salieron los muertos" and "En el cayo." However, *No sé quién soy* is less complex, developing a single narrative line divided into two sections.

The first paragraph of the story focuses on a specific detail, the hand of a young woman suspended in space and holding a pistol.

The second paragraph opens to a more extensive view and presents the girl and the body of her dead lover. These two paragraphs are brief and center on specific aspects of exterior reality. The third paragraph is much more extensive and moves to the point of view of an omniscient narrator who emphasizes exterior reality, but who also enters the thoughts of the young woman. The author uses the first three paragraphs to move from a narrow and specific aspect of reality to an expanded presentation. This procedure moves the reader from a puzzling fact to a comprehensive understanding of what is taking place—an effective way to capture a reader's attention.

From this point on the author assumes the role of an omniscient narrator who moves back and forth between exterior reality and the inner thoughts of the protagonist. The young woman, Minerva, had been involved in a suicide pact with an older, married man; but after shooting her lover she is seized by a psychic and emotional trauma and does not carry through with her part of the plan. Her emotional turmoil is slowly matched by the gradual onset of a hurricane, and as the storm's intensity increases, the story becomes a chronicle of her struggle for survival. Most of the work is devoted to the destructive force of the hurricane which operates as an exterior manifestation of Minerva's psychic disintegration and loss of orientation. As the storm rages on, Minerva is unable to distinguish between the land and the sea, and all distinctions disappear in a blinding and deafening movement of air and objects. The increase in the hurricane's destructive strength is matched by Minerva's descent into irrationality and madness, and she loses all sense of personal identity. Minerva is finally picked up by an ambulance and taken to a hospital where she continually repeats that she can no longer walk and doesn't know who she is. Her physical exhaustion parallels her emotional dissolution. The story ends with a return to an exterior presentation of reality, and Minerva's disorientation is controlled by a doctor's optimistic statement that they will restore her memory.

Novás Calvo employs in *No sé quién soy* essentially the same narrative procedure he used in "La noche de Ramón Yendía" of *La luna nona y otros cuentos*, and he continued this type of narration in "La visión de Tamaría" [The Vision of Tamaría] of *Cayo Canas*. However, *No sé quién soy* does not capture the reader in as compelling a manner as the other two stories, mainly because it centers more on the phenomenon of the hurricane rather than on the protagonist, and the reader almost becomes oblivious to human presence. To a certain extent, the raging storm becomes the true protagonist of most of *No sé quién soy* and this diminishes the work's dramatic impact. It was this stress on the hurricane that particularly attracted Fernando Ortiz's attention, for he was fascinated with the story's presentation of the supernatural significance of the hurricane, which he regarded as a manifestation of cosmic synergy.[3]

III *"La visión de Tamaría"*

Cayo Canas contains seven stories. Three of these works, "Un dedo encima," " 'Aliados' y 'Alemanes,' " and "El otro cayo" have been analyzed in previous chapters.[4] "La visión de Tamaría" is one of the outstanding selections in this volume and one of Novás Calvo's best stories. The narrator is similar to that of "La noche de Ramón Yendía" and the language flows effortlessly, creating the singular and solitary world of Andrés Tamaría through a number of sensorial suggestions. Narrated from the point of view of an omniscient narrator, "La visión de Tamaría" begins with a description of a powerful and superb swimmer moving with ease through the water.

He had plunged in from the deep shore cutting through the water, his deeply tanned back hardly visible in the afternoon sun: feet and legs like fins of imperceptible motion, one arm extended forward like an arrow, the other backwards like a side propeller, his head in front, opening the way like a prow, with his chin toward the sea. He advanced without fatigue or change, with implacable precision, hardly leaving a faint and thin, foamless wake that disappeared in an instant. For a few seconds he could be seen advancing with his head lined up with the background of the virgin beach: then, alone with the sea, he seemed motionless without any reference point, like a brighter speck of the blue-green mass, like a slight ripple, in the west, and finally he merged with the sea.[5]

The utilization of words such as "fins," "propeller," and "prow" convey the swimmer's strength, and his precise, tireless movement through the water scarcely leaves a wake, suggesting the precision and efficiency of his form. Andrés swims so far into the sea that he disappears from sight, a symbolic act of multiple meaning, for it denotes the solitary nature of his life and his movement into blindness. Also, it can be regarded as a premonition of what is to come.

We join Tamaría at sea in the next paragraph as he floats on the water and meditates, and the narrator uses this situation as a springboard from which he moves into the past and future. The initial paragraph presents Tamaría as others see him, but this exterior view quickly fades and we soon enter the sightless world of the protagonist. Sound and the sense of touch are particularly used and they serve, in effect, as reference points that Andrés employs to locate himself in time and space. As he floats at sea, for example, he knows the time of day by the angle of the sun's warm rays on his face. The noise of waves breaking on shore, the shouts of people frolicking on the beach, and the coolness and warmth of the water at different depths are indications of the many factors cited to convey Tamaría's world.

This technical procedure is utilized to relate a dramatic event that takes place one day while Tamaría, absorbed in thought, is floating in the ocean. He can hear the distant sounds of people on the beach and feels the sun on his face, and he drifts into a restful sense of security that is soon broken.

Not wanting to get any closer (there was now noise at the edge of the water), he rested face up, until he felt, lukewarm, the sun on his face. For a long time he remained engrossed and lost in thought. The din of the people on the outer edge of the shore sounded far-off and the gentle waves hardly moved him back and forth. This tranquility was instantly broken by a deep turbulence in the water. At first he supposed that it was a young shark or ray, among those that at times approached the beach too closely, but at once he felt the difference, although he hardly had time to do so mentally. A sort of underwater wave passed slightly touching him. For a few moments too tense to be measured, it circled him, passed under him, and in a bound, was on him. For a moment it had him in an embrace, adhered to him, covered him, like a wave, and, with the same suddenness it went off laughing toward the beach, with a giggle of curly and firm foam. (p. 84)

The rapid transitions from serenity to tenseness and fear, and then to relief and excited revelation are skillfully handled by a series of concrete references to the senses of sound and touch. The turbulence in the water strikes fear in Tamaría and the reader, especially when sharks and rays are mentioned, for these creatures awaken an instinctive sense of dread. These threatening omens are followed by further turmoil in the water around Tamaría and actual contact then takes place. This tense situation is broken by a laugh that signifies a human presence, and the implication that the person is feminine is conveyed by the reference to the "giggle of curly and firm foam"—an excellent synthesis of the aural and tactile. The sound of her voice is merged with suggestions that convey the sensation of brushing against her hair and soft but firm body. This unexpected and intimate contact with another human being is part of a series of events that drastically change Andrés's life.

Andrés Tamaría's blindness had stricken him as a youth and his adjustment to his condition is gradual, painful, and never complete. He lives on a beach and time for him is measured in seasons, particularly the arrival and departure of tourists, rather than days. The notion of time scarcely exists for Andrés since he lives in a world of darkness and is removed from light, the element most intimately related to our concept of time. Tamaría is torn between an overwhelming need to withdraw from people and a desire for human contact. He never resolves this contradiction, and it becomes a paradox in the unfolding of his life. Over the years a young woman who spends summers at the beach succeeds in breaking through some of Andrés's defenses and they become friends. The relationship, however, begins to deteriorate and one day, while searching for her in the water, Tamaría swims among bathers, a practice he had always avoided. He suddenly finds himself surrounded by unknown people, and he panics and swims out to sea in a frantic and undirected burst of energy. When he finally calms down, he realizes the sun is setting and that he has lost all sense of direction. The story becomes from this point a narration of Andrés's desperate efforts to return to land. Ironically, the sounds of human presence he had so often avoided become a necessity to his survival.

As fatigue and weariness slowly overwhelm him, Andrés reaches a stage where he thinks he can hear and see people on the beach. He makes a last desperate effort to reach shore and he even tries to call out for help, but the figures he sees and seeks dissolve. "Andrés clawed left and right, but on doing so, he noted that the person he thought he had grasped dissolved and he was sinking underneath the surface. Each time he clawed he sank more and more, out to sea, into the sea, further, each time further from shore, from its white beaches, toward the hidden darkness, toward the remote and underwater darkness . . ." (pp. 98-99). Andrés had lived in his own interior world for a long time, an introverted existence symbolized by his blindness. The reality of the exterior world finally invades his domain in the person of the young girl, and his death is a direct result of his attempt to exteriorize his emotions in his affection for her. It is ironic that his process of exteriorization results in his descent into the formless and dark depths of the sea.

"La visión de Tamaría" abounds in paradoxes. The blind Andrés dies in a state of hallucinatory vision, thinking he sees that which he is incapable of viewing. He seeks what he has always avoided, yet his desire for human warmth proves to be his undoing. The sea which was a refuge becomes his tomb, and his physical blindness is repeated and expanded as the blackness of the night and the sea envelop him. Andrés, who had always known where he was, who had thrived and guided himself by geometrical calculations, perishes swimming out to sea rather than toward land. The powerful swimmer whose hands and feet are like fins, dies clawing the water like a wretched animal who cannot swim. The blond and golden-tanned Andrés is victimized by one fatal flaw, his inability to deal with his blindness, and a young woman who seeks him out becomes the siren who precipitates his end. "La visión de Tamaría" is a story of paradoxical meanings, conveyed by a language of amazing vitality. It is an artistic work in which form, language, and content blend together into a harmonious balance of creative perfection.

Tamaría and the protagonist of "La noche de Ramón Yendía" provoke their own deaths by their inability to control fear, and this irony is central to the experience of both stories. Ramón's panic is instigated by his own guilt and the disintegration of the social order around him, but Tamaría wages an individual and personal battle against his own condition. Tamaría's struggle is with himself and his fear of rejection by society, while Ramón is more a victim of social and political forces outside of his control. The important point is that the two men play an active role in creating the terror that sets in motion the final events of their lives, and despite the importance of external forces they hold the key to their final fates.

IV "*Cayo Canas*"

The individual's struggle against fear is an important motif in the works of Novás Calvo, and the battle to maintain emotional stability in the face of adversity is a central concern. Novás Calvo utilizes the image of a steadily enclosing circle in some of his stories to convey the intense emotions of characters who feel trapped. This image is woven into the narrative fabric of "Un dedo encima" to capture the terror experienced by a young boy who is hunted like an animal by a neighborhood gang. The intended victim resorts to violence to break out of the circle closing in on him, but the protagonist of the title story of *Cayo Canas* is not as fortunate.

"Cayo Canas" opens with a reference that captures the great extension of space that the sea represents and this is combined with a threatening forewarning of what is to come. "The first one to see *them* was the boy, from the crow's nest, with his sharp eyes. They were still three dark points on the gray mass of the sea, but in the skipper's mind they instantly formed the tips of a spider's legs."[6] Oquendo, the protagonist of the story, finds himself being pursued by Hines, a former partner in smuggling. It is a deadly and unequal contest with Oquendo aboard a sailboat trying to evade several motor launches. Hines's squadron is sighted far off in the distance as mere specks on the horizon, but for Oquendo the dots are converted into the form of a spider. This image is extremely powerful for just as a spider weaves a concentric web to capture its victims, so does Hines circle in on Oquendo, forming a trap from which he cannot escape. As a weaver of death, Hines symbolizes the world of phenomena and its ceaseless process of change and destruction.

Sensing his inability to escape, Oquendo separates from his crew and members of his family in an effort to facilitate their escape. He sends them off in a small boat and rigs the sailboat to act as a decoy. Oquendo takes refuge on a small island, and the sea's limitless extension is now converted into a circle of water that makes escape impossible. Hines eventually realizes what has happened and sets different sections of the island on fire. Surrounded by an enclosing circle of flames, Oquendo's struggle now becomes one against his own terror. He devises plans that are never carried out and vacillates between acceptance and rejection of his fate, and the story becomes a study of the psychology of a trapped human facing the inevitability of death. A secondary theme is the blind struggle to survive that seizes all the animal and insect life on the isolated island, and this forms part of the process that reduces Oquendo to the most elemental aspects of his being.

The enclosing circle serves to intensify the limits of time and space that Oquendo faces, and furnishes an example of Novás Calvo's use of geometrical lines or progressions to create special effects. His geometrical configurations may have a precise and complete form as in the circles of "Cayo Canas" or "Un dedo encima"; they can be partial and intuitive like the arcs and angles that orient the blind swimmer in "La visión de Tamaría"; they may be labyrinthine and conveyed by random movement as in "La noche de Ramón Yendía," or take on the circular destructive form of a swirling hurricane that wreaks destruction and chaos in works like "En el cayo" and *No sé quién soy*. This variety of geometrical forms serves to convey the relationship between time and space and human destiny, and they are also employed to define the emotional state of characters. Death may be symbolized in Novás Calvo's stories by a closed, hermetic situation such as that of "Cayo Canas," or it may open up to a more extensive view like the merging with the formlessness of the sea in "La visión de Tamaría." These geometrical patterns enhance the structure of Novás Calvo's stories and contribute to the embodiment of meaning in form.

V *"No le sé desil"*

At the end of "La luna nona" and *No sé quién soy* an ambulance appears as a harbinger of death or symbol of futility after a violent act or psychological disintegration has taken place. This special vehicle occupies a more prominent role in "No le sé desil" [I Don't Know What to Say] and becomes the most important presence in the story. A doctor arrives with an ambulance in a rural area and establishes an emergency station, but when a patient dies in the vehicle, it is no longer regarded in the popular imagination as a source of help but as a place to die. Thereafter the ambulance's presence in the countryside only inspires fear and horror: "The white image passed like a white flash of heat lightning, over the hard roads, leaving behind a trail of terror."[7] One day the doctor is asked to help two men who have been involved in a violent conflict, and he makes a frantic effort to reach them before they bleed to death. Most of the story describes his struggle to drive the ambulance through muddy roads and his desperation and frustration with the slowness of the trip. The wives of the two men accompany the doctor and their strange calmness contrasts with the doctor's exasperation. At the end of the story the doctor discovers, along with the reader, that he has only been summoned to transport dead bodies, and this ironic revelation reveals the uselessness of technological advances in the face of superstition. The story's development focuses on the effect produced by the doctor's realization that he has been exploited in a manner he could scarcely have anticipated.

VI "¡Trínquenme ahí a ese hombre!"

"¡Trínquenme ahí a ese hombre!" [Tie That Man Down!] is the shortest narration in *Cayo Canas*, and its length scarcely reaches two thousand words. Guillermo Cabrera Infante parodied the style of several Cuban writers in one section of his novel *Tres Tristes Tigres* (1967) [Three Trapped Tigers], and his imitation of Novás Calvo is patterned on this story. Despite its brevity, "¡Trínquenme ahí a ese hombre!" is a significant work, and its seemingly candid and direct narration belies its complexity. It marks Novás Calvo's initial use of a narrative technique that formed the basis of stories published in the 1960s and 1970s, such as "El hombre-araña" [The Spider Man] and "La vaca en la azotea" [The Cow on the Rooftop]. "¡Trínquenme ahí a ese hombre!" is the first story that Novás Calvo wrote in which the reader has cause to doubt the veracity of the narrator's version of events, and since the work is presented in the first-person singular, we depend entirely on his account.

As the story opens, the narrator is exhorting others to securely tie up an old man who has just attacked him, a conflict the speaker evidently lost. "If he hadn't been crazy . . . I didn't know. One doesn't fight with a crazy man: it's like fighting against two, the man and his madness."[8] The assailant attempted to settle accounts for wrongs the narrator claims he had nothing to do with, and he proceeds to set the record straight, particularly for the benefit of his attacker. He begins his account by insisting on his respectablility and trustworthiness, referring to his standing in the community to assure his listeners of his credibility. He then relates his version of the events that led to the attack and explains that it all began a year ago.

At that time his assailant's wife was seriously ill and bedridden, and the old man brought in a young girl, Tulita, supposedly to care for the wife. However, Tulita is somewhat of a flirt, and the old man and the narrator begin entertaining amorous intentions. The ill wife recognizes what is going on, tells Tulita she wishes to meet her husband's hired hand, and suggests to Tulita that the young man is very handsome. The narrator implies that despite her serious illness, the wife, through a great effort of will, lingered on to see events take their course. Although there are never any indications of a romantic relationship between Tulita and the hired hand, according to the narrator, they run off one night after stealing the old man's hidden money. They are never seen again, and the old man, concluding that the narrator has killed the hired hand and carried off the girl, attacks him.

There are a number of indications that the narrator had been seriously interested in Tulita. He vividly describes her sensuality, indicates that she flirted with him, tells of his friends' teasing him about her, relates how the old man repeatedly told him to stay away, and explains he left the community because he realized he had no chance of success with Tulita and could not stand seeing her. His departure, it seems, coincides with the disappearance of the girl and the hired hand. But what causes the reader to have serious doubts about his story is that he knows more than he should about what happened. He reports on conversations that took place between Tulita and the sick woman and literally quotes what was said; he knew about the hidden money, and tells how Tulita and the hired hand discovered the old man's cache. In short, he has information that (most likely) could have come only from Tulita. We cannot know what really happened, although there is enough evidence to construct various conjectures. The narrator appears to be more deeply involved in the events than he reveals and we wonder if the old man's rage and madness are caused by psychological disintegration or by frustration spurred on by the narrator's tormenting and vindictive tone. The storyteller's scornful treatment of the old man may be partly a result of his injured pride, but also partly a projection of guilt. The story opens and closes on a shrill tone that conveys the narrator's apprehension and tenseness, and the flow of the first person narrative has a confessional tinge at times. When the narrator states that Tulita and the hired hand separately followed and observed the old man go to his cache one evening, we ask how he knows this and question his role in the matter. "¡Trínquenme ahí a ese hombre!" leaves the reader pondering a number of contingencies and untangling possible contradictions.

VII *A Decline in Activity*

The first six years of the 1940s formed the most significant period of Novás Calvo's literary career. The later years of that decade marked the beginning of a decline in activity that evolved into a period of dormancy that lasted until 1961. During 1947 and 1948 two fragments of a novel, "Los Oquendo" [The Oquendo Family], appeared in a Mexican journal, but the work was never finished.[9]

These selections are interesting because the author employs a first-person narration to allow a woman to reveal herself to the reader. The setting of this work is the same as that of "La noche de Ramón Yendía," the waning period of the Machado dictatorship in 1933, and the narration is from the point of view of a woman whose cynical husband is a calculating informer. She resorts to murder to protect her husband, but feels no compassion for her victim although he is a former lover. In another episode she suspects her husband may be taking his life and that of their son, but she feels no compulsion to act. The dangerous struggle for survival has caused her to develop the capacity to alienate herself from her own feelings, and she becomes a deadened human being. This concern had appeared previously in *El negrero* and "La primera lección," among others, but in these fragments of "Los Oquendo" there is recognition and contemplation of the condition, an element that did not exist before.

Two additional stories were published in 1948 and 1951 in *Orígenes*, a journal edited by the distinguished Cuban poet and novelist, José Lezama Lima.[10] "El cuarto de morir" [A Room for Dying] concerns the indifferent and cruel treatment the young sometimes visit on the aged. This story, which appeared in 1948, contains a narrative pattern that occurs frequently in Novás's stories—centering around the individual who does not belong or fit into a particular social situation. In this case, an eighty-seven-year-old woman, Anselma, finds herself an outcast among members of her own family and becomes the victim of their indifference, resentment, and hate. The tragedy of the situation is intensified by the fact that Anselma has two sons, but they are too involved in their own lives and needs to devote much time or patience to Anselma, and they choose not to expend much effort or concern on her. She discovers that the invitation she received to live with one of her sons was not an act of love, but merely a means to make his brother look bad. The narration is omniscient and fluctuates between two predominant points of view, those of the narrator and Anselma. This binary narrative mode presents the reader with a sufficiently complete panorama of events and allows him to see some episodes from the perspective of the story's victim, Anselma.

The emotional reality of "El cuarto de morir" is stark and unvarnished; there is little room in this tragedy of human relationships for generosity or kindness. Anselma is no longer useful to anyone, and she has become a cantankerous burden to her family. She feels completely abandoned, for even the prayers she directs at the saints and God asking for vengeance go unheeded. Anselma's sons finally rent a room in a neighboring home for her; and after a heavy rain she spends a few days trapped by a flooded patio. Enclosed by water and neglected by those who should care, Anselma's physical isolation symbolizes the reality of her tragic circumstance. We last see her experiencing the final and nearly imperceptible convulsions of death, unattended and brushed aside by the granddaughter who is sent to deliver a piece of cake. "El cuarto de morir" is one of Novás Calvo's most pessimistic works, and it is unrelenting in its presentation of the darker and more tragic aspects of family relationships.

The story that appeared in 1951, "A ese lugar donde me llaman" [The Place That's Calling Me], presents a child's gradual comprehension of his mother's approaching death. This story is superior to "El cuarto de morir" and its success depends on the skillful combination of two entirely different attitudes toward the tragic events—the child's innocent, emotional incomprehension and the mother's fearful and protective desire to avoid the inevitable for the sake of her child. The mother clings to the hope that the boy's absent father will return before her death and assume responsibility for their son's care. Since the child is illegitimate, the mother and her son are barely accepted by society and she is even shunned by her own family. The arrival of ships in port is preceded by the exaltation that conveys her hope that the father will return and is inevitably followed by the depression and sorrow of each disappointment. The changes in her emotional state parallel the fluctuations in her physical health, but her condition deteriorates to the point that even the child realizes she is dying. The mother finally concludes that her expectations are futile and leaves for a hospital where she knows she will die.

"A ese lugar donde me llaman" is narrated by the child who recalls the events prior to his final separation from his mother. The first sentence ("It all began—that's how I remember it—at the end of September") introduces a binary time frame that is developed throughout the story.[11] The use of the past tense ("it all began") and the present tense ("that's how I remember it") in the same sentence establishes the narrator's dual view of the events. The story is presented through the eyes of the narrator as a child, but there are commentaries made by the narrator as an older person who has acquired some insight and comprehension of the tragic circumstances. Although the child's incomprehension predominates, the retrospective presentation permits the reader to comprehend fully what is happening. Other characters, particularly the mother, are directly quoted, but we see the episodes through the eyes of the child. This perspective is used consistently in the story although there are a variety of speakers.

The situation is basically tragic, but the story ends on a positive note. The narrator remarks that time has slowly erased the image of the sickly, dying woman and replaced it with that of the vital and healthy figure she once was. In this regard, it is the essence of the woman's role as a mother that remains in the narrator's mind rather than her death, and human memory triumphs over adversity. This is underscored by the last words of the story, the reiteration of one of the mother's last wishes: "I don't want him to remember me ugly and worn out. I want him to remember me as I am . . . , as I was" (p. 74). The story concludes with the mother combining the past and present in one sentence just as the narrator did in the very first line of the work. This synthesis conveys the timeless aspect of human memory and its ability to overcome the barriers of time and circumstance.

Except for the publication of some journalistic crime stories in the popular magazine *Bohemia* during the 1950s, "A ese lugar donde me llaman" was followed by a period of inactivity that lasted until 1961.[12] Novás Calvo has had a long-standing interest in detective stories and he once stated that "the best composed structure is that of the detective novel."[13] The complicated intricacy of this type of writing fascinates him, and it is this element that most closely resembles the attention to form and detail that characterizes his own work.

Novás Calvo became a professor of French in the Teachers' School of Havana in 1947, but he temporarily lost this position in 1951 after a change in government. Salvador Bueno has described, in an essay written before the issue was settled, the psychological impact this episode had on Novás Calvo, and he pointed out that the situation had intensified all the insecurities that Novás Calvo's turbulent past had instilled in him.[14] Bueno presents a poignant picture of a man translating at his typewriter all day for *Bohemia* to supplement his income. Novás Calvo regained his post, but he had to prove his competency to a special review board.[15] A more pleasant event of this period was a request by Ernest Hemingway that he translate *The Old Man and the Sea* for a Spanish edition of *Life*. Novás Calvo's fee for this endeavor was a used Ford, an appropriate compensation for a writer whose own works frequently revealed his fascination with cars.[16] His only additional noteworthy literary publication of the 1950s was *El otro cayo* (1959) which consists of five stories from *La luna nona y otros cuentos* and *Cayo Canas*, but no new works were included. The volume contained "El otro cayo," "Cayo Canas," "No le sé desil," "Hombre malo," and "Long Island." Novás Calvo's artistic skills remained dormant until a cataclysmic event, the Cuban Revolution, shook and modified the foundations of Cuban society.

CHAPTER 6

The Revolutionary Period

I *The Reluctant Fugitive*

THOSE who have the good fortune to live long lives discover that longevity also has its disadvantages, for certain tragedies such as the death of friends and intimates occur all too frequently. Some individuals must also confront difficulties that fall outside the scope of those who lead more mundane existences. Both of these circumstances have been Novás Calvo's fate. His mother could scarcely have known when she sent her seven-year-old son to Cuba from Spain that she was setting into motion a pattern that would be repeated. Novás Calvo's difficult childhood and youth was followed by a fruitful return to Spain in 1931, but this period came to an unpleasant end when the Spanish Republic ceased to exist in 1939. He fled to France and returned destitute to Cuba, but then embarked on the most successful years of his life. However, in 1960 events took another fateful turn for Novás Calvo.

During the first months of that year he was a member of a panel of judges in the first Spanish-American literary contest sponsored by the Casa de las Américas. He served with Miguel Angel Asturias, Antonio Ortega, and Virgilio Piñera and evaluated contestants in the short story.[1] However, when the editor of *Bohemia*, Miguel Angel Quevedo, clashed with Fidel Castro and his revolutionary government, Novás Calvo found himself implicated, and after receiving warnings that he was about to be arrested, he sought and received political asylum in the Colombian Embassy.[2] After a two-month stay in the embassy, he left for the United States in September 1960.

Novás Calvo's eight-month stay in the United States in 1926 had not been pleasant, but his second visit and residence was more fruitful. He worked as an assistant editor for the Cuban exile magazine *Bohemia Libre* in New York City for two years, and when that magazine moved to Caracas, Venezuela, he became an employee of *Vanidades*, a women's journal edited by his wife, Herminia del Portal. *Vanidades* was eventually sold to Venezuelan interests and Novás Calvo then joined the staff of the Department of Romance Languages of Syracuse University as a visiting professor of Spanish. He taught at that institution from 1967 until 1974 when he retired after suffering a stroke. His friends and admirers at Syracuse University organized a special colloquium in his honor on his retirement. His period of teaching at Syracuse University was particularly satisfying for he was surrounded by colleagues who enjoyed and esteemed his presence.

II A Renewed Career: The Stories of 1961–1963

Although abandoning Cuba was a traumatic personal event, it did have the salutary effect of provoking the renewal of Novás Calvo's literary career. His first creative effort in several years, "Con un nudo en el corazón" [With a Heavy Heart], was published in the December 24, 1961, issue of *Bohemia Libre*.[3] The narration is a retrospective view of the disintegration of a family and its happy reconciliation during the Christmas season. The narrator, who was seven years old when the events of the story took place, recounts his memories of that particular holiday season. Although the narrator is now an adult, most of the story is presented through the eyes of a young child. The narrator speaks, but it is the child who sees— a technique that Novás Calvo frequently employs.

This tentative return to prose fiction was followed by five other stories that appeared in the pages of *Bohemia Libre* between 1961 and 1963.[4] Unlike "Con un nudo en el corazón," these five works deal with the Cuban Revolution and concern misdirected violence or vengeance. "Un buchito de café" [A Small Cup of Coffee] narrates how a rural family is mistakenly killed by nervous revolutionaries who think the family has attempted to poison them. "El milagro" [The Miracle] presents the creative and destructive influence of the Revolution on a professor and his wife—she overcomes a crippling condition, but he is unjustly hunted by a revolutionary seeking vengeance. In "Fernández al paredón" [The Execution of Fernández] an innocent policeman is executed by a firing squad headed by his illegitimate son who is unaware of the terrible significance of the event. As in many of Novás's revolutionary stories, the desire for revenge becomes a blind force that destroys friend and foe alike.

The message seems clear—when a man kills others, a part of his own intimate being also dies.

Although "Fernández al paredón" is narrated in omniscient third person, the point of view occasionally fluctuates between that of the narrator and Fernández. This subtle technique is used very effectively in the final lines of the story which present the last figures that Fernández sees a moment before his death: "For an instant Fernández could still see, over the firing squad, the blurred outlines of the two women who were coming into view in the distance, and he had time only to think: Micaela, Amalia—before the volley sounded."[5] The two feminine figures are his wife and the mother of his illegitimate son. Fernández dies in the presence of the most significant people in his life, including the son who oversees his death, and a web of fatal circumstances draws to a tragic close. "Fernández al paredón" is one of the more successful revolutionary stories of the 1961–1963 period.

III *"La abuela reina y el sobrino Delfín"*

The distinction between reality and fantasy is not always clear to the reader in the next two stories that appeared in *Bohemia Libre*— "La abuela reina y el sobrino Delfín" [The Grandmother Queen and Her Nephew Delfín] and "El hombre-araña" [The Spider Man]. In both works the narrator is perplexed by a turn of events and the reader is left with the responsibility of reaching his own conclusions about the stories. "La abuela reina y el sobrino Delfín" is presented in the form of a letter sent from Cuba to a family member in the United States. María tells her sister in New York of the gradual disintegration of their family as the Revolution moves into their lives. María's style is direct and informal: "You're going to have to prepare yourself to read this letter. You're going to cry, moan, get mad, maybe laugh a little. It's taken me weeks to write you, at night, hidden, almost without light, in the section of the house they left us in the garden."[6]

María relates the sad fate of many relatives, but one, a great-aunt, resists in a half-crazed fashion. The old woman is somewhat reminiscent of the mother in "Un dedo encima." The two women are outcasts and the objects of scorn and ridicule, and they both predict that dire consequences will befall their tormentors. The old woman of "La abuela reina y el sobrino Delfín" claims that a nephew will appear with his brothers to avenge the treatment she is receiving.

In her constant ravings she almost converts her nephew into a mythological figure, one who doesn't smoke or drink, and who protects and defends those who are persecuted. Even María confesses that "I myself began to have doubts that he was a man of flesh and blood, although I knew that we had some cousins with those names" (p. 134).

To the astonishment of the narrator and the reader, Delfín and his brothers do appear, the predicted vengeance is meted out, and five men are killed by machetes. María explains that the whole episode "lasted hardly an instant," and that at its conclusion the old woman and her avengers "dissolved into the darkness" (p. 149). María closes her letter without any further explanations of the event and subtly shifts the responsibility of deciding what actually happened to her reader. "Now you see what I mean, sister! For the time being, I've got nothing more to tell you. I leave you with grandmother and her nephews Delfín, Santos, and Servando: wherever they may be" (p. 149). Like the sister to whom the letter is addressed, the reader is left with the necessity of interpreting events and deciding whether the version is nothing more than fantasy. It is an effective technique that greatly enhances the artistry of the story.

The language is the most engaging element in "La abuela reina y el sobrino Delfín." It flows easily and naturally, and is very convincing. Seymour Menton has pointed out that this story "probably would have been better as a novel. Rather than concentrating on one individual, which he does in most of his better stories, Novás presents the disintegration of an entire family during the first three years of the revolutionary government."[7] This observation is well taken for there are many characters in the work that hinder the story's development. Another detraction is the markedly anti-revolutionary stance of the story.

IV "El hombre-araña"

"El hombre-araña" was the last story to appear in *Bohemia Libre* and it shares many characteristics with "La abuela reina y el sobrino Delfín." The narrator, Pincho Peláez, speaks to a friend from a hospital bed in Miami shortly after his escape from Cuba. Pincho attempts to sort out the events of his life in an effort to understand what has happened to him, and his emotional intensity increases as he relives the past: "I'm talking to you as if the past were today."[8]

Pincho tells how his wife was transformed by the Revolution and of his murder of her lover. He is tried for his act and condemned to death, but he escapes with the help of friends. As he leaves the island by boat, he believes that he sees his wife with the man he had killed, a vision which continually torments him. "Even so, I am still fascinated by that mystery, because I don't understand how there can be two identical figures, two identical scenes, in an identical place on an identical night" (p. 316). The repetition of a key word in this quotation conveys the redundant and obsessive quality of his thoughts.

Others take the event as an hallucination or a case of mistaken identity, but Pincho cannot resolve the issue for he does not understand why the bullets that slayed his wife's lover did not kill her also. Pincho is the only one who believes his version of the final scene on the beach, although he claims to have witnesses. It is as if a nightmare has become a living reality for the harried narrator, whose obsessed mind will not let go of the past. The title of the story conveys his dread and apprehension; the unnamed lover is nicknamed for his long legs and arms, and in spider-like fashion weaves a web of intrigue and illusion from which Pincho's possessed mind cannot escape.

If the reader wishes, he can regard the story as a metaphor of a vision of existence. The image of the spider can be taken as an agent of destruction and change—a part of the ceaseless forces of existence. And within this scheme, death is just another thread in the many patterns of life which connect the old with the new. It is significant that the bizarre events of "El hombre-araña" take place in the moonlight, a fact Pincho mentions several times. J. E. Cirlot has pointed out that "the moon, since it holds sway over the whole phenomenal world (for all phenomenal forms are subject to growth and death), weaves the thread of each man's destiny. Accordingly, the moon is depicted as a gigantic spider in many myths."[9]

It could be that Pincho vaguely senses the significance of the unusual episodes, but he is unable to fathom their meaning or communicate their significance to those around him. His feverish ramblings convey the inner tensions of a mind that has glimpsed patterns of existence that are too terrible to accept. Pincho resorts to violence in a frantic effort to resolve his difficulties, but he has essentially lost control of his life. In this regard, what actually happens in the story is less important than the narrator's psychological reactions to what he perceives. For example, the spider-like figure is indestructible in Pincho's mind because it is an incarnation of the revolutionary process.

The mixture of fantasy and reality in the mind of the narrator is an important ingredient in "El hombre-araña" and "La abuela reina y el sobrino Delfín," and this literary device enhances the artistry of these particular stories. This technique was used with great success several years later in "Mi tío Antón Luna" [My Uncle Antón Luna] and "La vaca en la azotea" [The Cow on the Rooftop]—two of the most outstanding stories of Novás Calvo's revolutionary period. Although "El hombre-araña" and "La abuela reina y el sobrino Delfín" share an anti-revolutionary stance, it is less pronounced in the first-named story. Revolutionary elements are more convincingly incorporated into a narrative pattern that centers on the ceaseless process of change in "El hombre-araña." The story is a vision of the revolutionary process as perceived by those who are swept away by its profound changes.

V *The Stories from* Bohemia Libre *in* Maneras de contar

The five stories from *Bohemia Libre* that deal with the Revolution were republished in 1970 in *Maneras de contar* [Narrative Modes], and one of them, "Un buchito de café," was changed considerably in the second version and is presented as if it were a tape recording. A young man who survived the slaughter of several members of his family by revolutionaries obsessively relates what happened to four strangers. It is implied that the four are the murderers, and they leave bowed and overwhelmed by their guilt. The changes improve the story and one can regard the revision as an indication that the deep passions provoked by Novás Calvo's loss of his country were beginning to subside. His revolutionary stories focus on the illogical course of human events and the profound tragedies that occur when conflict polarizes men. When individuals become mortal enemies, they are converted into dehumanized objects marked for extermination in a system where justice disappears. Although some interesting biographical details are included in these stories (the seekers of vengeance in "El milagro" and "Fernández al paredón" are named Carmona and Nenclares, an obvious reflection of the Carmona Nenclares who falsely accused Novás Calvo during the Spanish Civil War), there is a decided absence of a presentation of the emotional experience of being an exile. This condition is alluded to in several stories, but its emotional and psychological significance is never directly confronted. Like the episodes of the Spanish Civil War, the ordeal of losing one's country was apparently too painful and immediate an event to be rendered into artistic expression.[10]

VI *Two Stories of 1965*

The preoccupation with revenge is present in Novás Calvo's next two stories, both of 1965, but the scene shifts to the conflicts between Cuban exiles in the United States.[11] As successive waves of Cubans sought refuge in this country, many discovered that they were being joined in exile by countrymen who had once been agents of the Revolution, and Novás Calvo's stories deal with individuals who decide to settle old scores. "La noche en que Juan tumbó a Pedro" [The Night That Juan Destroyed Pedro] returns to an approach utilized in *Un experimento en el Barrio Chino* of 1936. Like the rich woman of that novelette, one of the characters of this story experiments with other people's lives. He arranges a supposedly chance meeting between two mortal enemies to see what will happen, and his manipulative cynicism is not disappointed with the results.

"Un 'bum' " [A 'Bum'] narrates one exile's murder of another in New York City, and the story enters the thoughts of the avenger so the reader witnesses his manipulation of his victim and his adroit concealment of his true feelings until a decisive and sudden move is made. Tension is skillfully increased in the story by the reader's expectation of violence. When the discovery of the victim's body is reported in a newspaper, it is assumed he is a bum who died an accidental death. The story, therefore, closes on a note that completely denies the victim's identity and concludes with his total dehumanization. If the reader identifies with the murderer, and the story is designed in part to procure this effect, he may find himself vaguely troubled by pangs of conscience. In fact, the narration contains an ambivalence that produces contradictory emotions in the reader.

This ambivalence is created by a number of polarities that exist in the text. Jorge Pallares, the murderer, is a picture of strength and aggressive vitality while his victim, who has recently arrived from Cuba, is a weak and an emotionally exhausted man. As the two men walk through a deserted area of New York City on a cold Sunday they pass frozen cats and dogs, but Pallares points out historical sites related to José Martí and George Washington, men who are abstract symbols of the ideal. The ugly reality of the area and the bleakness of the wintry scene contrast with the lofty idealism represented by Martí and Washington and the men's feigned friendship. When Pallares finally kills his old enemy, he experiences a tremendous sense of relief which counters the repulsive nature of the murder. Pallares also toys with his victim as a cat plays with a mouse, and the author suggests the cruelty of his actions. There are other polarities in the text that produce contradictory feelings in the reader, and Pallares's complete lack of remorse intensifies this uneasiness. In his introduction to this story Novás Calvo pointed out that the plot is based on what an exiled friend would have liked to have done, and that he told Novás Calvo after reading the story that "the intention was mine, but the crime is yours,"[12] an apt indication of the ambivalence so successfully conveyed in the story.

VII Maneras de contar *and the Stories of 1968–1973*

Novás Calvo's last collection of short stories, *Maneras de contar*, appeared in 1970, and of the eighteen stories in the volume, thirteen deal with the Revolution and were written after the author came to the United States. The other five stories in the collection are earlier pieces from different periods in his career.[13] Between 1968 and 1973 Novás Calvo also published several new stories in diverse journals and *Maneras de contar*, but only four of them concern the Revolution.[14] This change in emphasis was accomplished by a decided improvement in the quality of the stories, regardless of their subject matter. It is interesting to note that the revelation of the identity of a character is an important process in several of these works.

In "Nadie a quien matar" [No One to Kill] and "Peor que un infierno" [Worse Than a Hell] the identity of the narrator is not disclosed until the end of the story, and in both instances the speaker turns out to be an important participant in the work's development. This discovery surprises the reader for he has the impression throughout most of the story that the speaker's version is fairly objective since he appears to be an observer rather than an active participant. The revelation that the narrator is an active participant in the events causes the reader to question the veracity of the version he has read and to reevaluate the entire story.

"Peor que un infierno" is based on a crime story, "Angusola y los cuchillos" [Angusola and the Knives], that Novás Calvo published years earlier in the popular Cuban magazine *Bohemia*. He has stated that he doubts if "the reconstruction is very similar to the original," but he has admitted that "perhaps it conserves the tone, atmosphere, some of the characters and part of the theme" of the earlier version.[15] The narrative form of this story is particularly interesting. Most of the work creates the impression that an omniscient narrator is relating a tale of crime and passion, but the reader is offered a series of clues that indicate that this is not the case. For example, the supposedly omniscient narrator suddenly uses the first-person singular in one instance to indicate that he does not know what motivated one of the characters to initiate a particular course of action. In addition, the second paragraph which is enclosed in parentheses, presents a brief first-person narration that asks the reader's indulgence for what he is about to hear. "(I am sorry that I have to tell this story. It's something that shouldn't be said. Because of this I beg your pardon. One shouldn't find out about such things, but when he comes across them, he has to relate them. They are too terrible to be kept secret!)."[16] Since the reader does not know who the speaker is and the narrator implies that a horrible tale is about to be told, this aside stimulates curiosity. The only other time this technique is used is at the very end of the story, which closes with the following declaration: "I am really sorry to have had to tell this story. There is one thing that a real man should never do, and that is to speak badly of his woman, even though her name is Adelfa Rubio and she has a past like the one I have related. I'm sorry and I beg your pardon. But at times there are things that a man has to say, because they are too horrible to keep secret" (p. 26).

There is a slight shift in tone between the two declarations. The second is more resigned and less anxious, an indication, perhaps, that the narrator has relieved some of his inner tension and anguish by relating his tale of woe. The closing statement takes the reader by surprise for he realizes that the narrator is an important character in the work. This revelation clears up a number of loose ends in "Peor que un infierno" and the web of intricate relations that comprise the plot is disclosed. Nevertheless, some issues are left unsettled, and the identity of the perpetrator of a rape is left unresolved. Since the narrator's identity is revealed to the reader and we learn that he is an important participant in the story's development, we assume that the narrator cannot be fully trusted. One thing is left very clear, the narrator is victimized by his own arrogance and weakness. Although he knows that Adelfa's involvement with another young man resulted in his death, he does not hesitate to take up with her and her shady family. He knows, for example, that Adelfa's father killed the young man when her suitor attempted to terminate his relationship with her. In fact, the narrator had advised the young suitor to flee. When this counsel is accepted, it only results in the suitor's death. Nevertheless, the narrator once thought he could handle the situation. In an unusually candid statement the narrator refers to himself in the third person and admits that he was a perfect cynic who had faith in no one. *"He didn't believe in anyone.* He didn't love Adelfa in order to marry her and he didn't adore her like a Virgin. Furthermore, he was a rambling man who knew his way around, and he wasn't going to let himself be taken by surprise by the butcher's knife. So while he continued wooing Adelfa, he kept thinking about the secret duel he was waging against her father" (p. 24). This cynicism and arrogance prove to be his undoing and he succumbs to her charms and the threatening presence of her father. He rationalizes that Adelfa must have used some secret spell on him, for "the idea that it might be out of fear of Mario Rubio was too humiliating to be admitted" (p. 26). The narrator finds himself married to a promiscuous woman and a member of a family he can never leave except by death. The intricacy of the plot, the clever narrative devices, and the exceptional employment of colloquial language contribute to the success of "Peor que un infierno." The use of a narrator who evidently does not reveal all of the circumstances and implications of his story reminds one of the earlier work "¡Trínquenme ahí a ese hombre!" [Tie That Man Down!] Both stories tend to conceal complicated plots under the guise of what appears to be a straightforward narration, and in the two works the reader must question the reliability of the narrator in order to understand all of the story's implications.

A similar situation exists in "El esposo invisible" [The Invisible Husband] for the narrator's intimate knowledge of events arouses suspicions in the reader. Chago, the narrator, relates his tale with wit and cynicism and his skeptical tone contributes greatly to the success of the story. Chago is a journalist who has spent time as a social reporter and his profession gives him access to many people. He begins his tale by directly addressing his reader. "As you all know, I never was anything more than a reporter. I was many other things; but more than a reporter, nothing of the sort."[17] These first statements set up a pattern on which the story is based because the narrator begins by negatively asserting what he has been. This process of negative assertion establishes a pattern of affirmation and denial that characterizes the narrator's personality. He relates the story of Pepito Martínez but conceals important information from his audience, particularly any references to his participation in any crucial action in the story. When Pepito Martínez approaches him with a direct accusation, Chago's response is a typically expected denial which conforms to the central pattern in the story. The reader, however, gradually becomes aware of this process and by the end of the work has arrived at his own conclusions about the identity of a rapist and Chago's role in the whole strange tale.

Pepito Martínez is a man from a very modest background, but he is married to one of the stars of high society. His wife, Cecilia Valdés, is wealthy and extremely beautiful, and most individuals cannot understand how Pepito has managed to marry her.[18] The narrator approaches his story somewhat indirectly by way of his conversations with a psychiatrist who has treated Cecilia during three decisive periods of her life. Chago lists the psychiatrist's version of events and then proceeds to correct this information. "Cecilia, of course, had lied to him. She didn't tell him, for example, that the business of the hooded man wasn't a dream, but a reality; that her first bout with melancholy had been caused precisely by that. The only thing that did appear certain was that, contrary to appearances, Cecilia wasn't happy, since she was incapable of responding to her husband" (p. 395).

The narrator then proceeds to describe the strange occurrence of Cecilia's first sexual experience and how she was accosted by a hooded man who seduced her with words and emotion as much as by force.

No one had ever spoken to Cecilia Valdés like that. Later, when in their shameless dialogues other married women of high society spoke of how much their loss of virginity had hurt them, Cecilia never ceased being surprised. For her it had been like a long and pleasurable sigh that was then reproduced in dreams almost every night. The man who had assaulted Cecilia Valdés disappeared like he had come. Like a shadow. He had loved her, he had spoken sweetly in her ear. He hadn't hurt her, because those words had been like a drug. (p. 396)

Cecilia makes a considerable effort to identify her assailant by trying to recognize his voice among men she knows, but Chago points out that "it never occurred to her to think that a person can have one voice when he loves and another very different in other circumstances" (p. 396). At this point the reader begins to suspect that the narrator knows much more than he should, but Chago counters this suspicion by stating that Cecilia began to tell her psychiatrist the truth and that her doctor shared this information with him, even allowing Chago to listen to tapes of their sessions.

Some months after their marriage Pepito and Cecilia realize they have serious problems and they begin to search for solutions. Pepito begins to approach Chago with his dilemma, always by speaking indirectly of his own situation. The narrator understands what is happening and plays the game until Pepito tells him during a social gathering, "Chago, you know a lot. But you don't know one thing: the extremes of the sadness of having a frigid wife" (p. 400). And Chago reacts significantly: "I smiled at him with an irony that greatly intrigued him" (p. 400). Pepito finally tells Chago that he suspects that he is the rapist which Chago denies, but he does give Pepito a solution to his problem and even points out that "there is also a voice to cultivate" (p. 404). Just when the reader concludes that he understands what has happened, Chago closes his story by saying that Pepito and Cecilia have solved their marital problems, but that the rumors that a hooded man was seen around their home when Pepito was absent were false. The story, therefore, concludes with the same pattern of affirmation and denial with which it began, leaving the reader to puzzle over Chago's negative assertions. In any event, Chago's intimate knowledge of events arouses suspicions and at the conclusion of the story the reader has no doubts that the narrator is the unnamed villain.

"El esposo invisible" and "Peor que un infierno" were first published in 1969 and 1966 respectively, and they share some important characteristics. The two works present an episode involving an unidentified rapist whose attack profoundly influences his victim's personality. In both works Novás Calvo splits one character into two components, and the reader at first is not aware that this is taking place. In both instances a narrator speaks of himself in the third person in order to conceal his identity, and the discovery of this process is central to the reader's experience and to the dynamics of the story. In "Peor que un infierno" the narrator is victimized by his own arrogance, but we never discover the true motivations of the narrator's actions in "El esposo invisible." "Peor que un infierno" has a confessional tone, and the narrator reveals his true feelings and fate, but the storyteller of "El esposo invisible" never ceases to play with his listener. The cynical and comic stance he assumes remains the same throughout the story. We can question his motivations and actions, but his true intentions and feelings remain obscured by the sardonic mask he presents to the world. Both narrators are manipulative and evasive and this intensifies the impact of the unexpected endings.

There is a progressive development in the employment of a narrator who has a negative function in "Peor que un infierno," "Nadie a quien matar," and "El esposo invisible." In the first mentioned story the narrator simply brings about his own ruin, but in "El esposo invisible" the storyteller has a negative as well as positive influence on the other characters and the work's development. "Nadie a quien matar" is the most extreme application of this technique, and the narrator begins his story by demonstrating considerable respect for the subject of his tale and by insisting on the accuracy of his version of events. "This is the exact and true story of the last days of Lauro Aranguren. Pardon me: Dr. Lauro Aranguren, with all due respect."[19] After vaguely contradicting foreign versions of events (the action takes place in Cuba) and insisting again on the accuracy of his story by claiming that his version "is the most exact that a person can know" (p. 77) without being the actual person, he launches into his presentation. The narrator begins in this manner in order to gain the confidence of his reader, and his approach continues in this vein.

He tells of Lauro's difficulties with government authorities and how he was arrested and imprisoned without benefit of a legal process and claims he does not know why it happened this way. He does speculate about the possible causes, none of which are very favorable to the government, and then proceeds with his tale. The narrator relates a number of details of Lauro's life and his relationship with many members of his family, particularly an illegitimate half brother, Romilio. Lauro and Romilio have always been close and during Lauro's political difficulties Romilio is the one member of the family who consistently helps him. Lauro soon discovers that he is dying of an incurable disease and he decides to take vengeance on those who have caused his difficulties. His only problem is to identify them and carry out some kind of violent action.

After experiencing a number of frustrations and failures in his search for vengeance, Lauro decides to focus his hatred on the individual who is living in his confiscated house although he does not know who it is. Romilio tries to dissuade him from taking this course of action, but Lauro is now in such a frenzied emotional state that nothing can change his mind. He is compelled to act, to strike out somehow at those who have injured him. He seems to have forgotten that he and Romilio had agreed earlier that the important thing was to survive the social and political turmoil that was engulfing them and the country.

The narrator describes in minute detail Lauro's actions the evening he approaches his former home, carrying a revolver, determined to kill. In a description that recalls the use of circular imagery in "Un dedo encima" and "Cayo Canas," Lauro circles in on his target as if following the course of a secret destiny. "He was approaching, in circles, following an invisible spiral" (p. 88). Unfortunately for Lauro, someone in the house is awaiting him and he is killed by three shots from a firearm when he makes his move. At this point the reader discovers that Lauro's killer is Romilio, and it is soon revealed that Romilio is also the narrator. A number of clues interwoven into the text are now filled with meaning, particularly Romilio's basic decision to survive: "But you and I have always thought the same: one has to live. Isn't that true, brother?" (p. 83). There are also hints of Romilio's jealousy of the superior social position and home Lauro once enjoyed. The technique of using a narrator who conceals his identity and speaks of himself in the third person is combined in "Nadie a quien matar" with Novás Calvo's predilection for presenting characters who are instrumental in their own destruction.

Identity is also a central concern in "El secreto de Narciso Campana" [The Secret of Narciso Campana], but in this case it is a change of identity that gives the story its dynamic quality. Narciso Campana is a passive and weak man whom others use as a doormat until he experiences a fascinating transformation. One day while strolling by the sea he finds a wallet which contains a chauffeur's license. Presuming that the owner is dead, Narciso decides to use the license and rent a taxicab. He gradually acquires the personality of the former owner of the license and his personal fortunes greatly improve. The weak and indecisive Narciso is replaced by an active and sometimes dangerous man. "El secreto de Narciso Campana" contains a variation of a theme used in an earlier story, "Hombre malo." In both works an individual's life drastically changes when he embraces a code of conduct based on strength and survival rather than timidity and morality. However, unlike the protagonist of "Hombre malo," Narciso's transformation does not deprive him of the capacity to tolerate intimate relationships. There is little complexity in the narration of "El secreto de Narciso Campana" and the story's appeal relies heavily on its content. "Nadie a quien matar," "Peor que un infierno," and "El secreto de Narciso Campana" are much more dependent on narrative technique, a factor which enhances these particular works.

VIII *"Mi tío Antón Luna"*

Two of the stories of the 1968–1973 period, "Mi tío Antón Luna" [My Uncle Antón Luna] and "Hacia Donde se acuesta el sol" [Toward the Setting Sun] are exceptional works and another, "La vaca en la azotea," [The Cow on the Rooftop] compares favorably with Novás Calvo's best stories. "Mi tío Antón Luna" is a good-natured story narrated by a wily but endearing rascal. The author weaves many details from his own life into the fabric of the work. These include important dates, uncles and acquaintances from his restless youth, a reference to a street where he worked in a bookstore, and the name of a former associate, José Antonio Fernández de Castro, the director of the journal that sent Novás Calvo to Spain in 1931. Although the author gently chides Fernández de Castro's political beliefs ("charity was the opium of the poor"), he also pokes fun at his own profession.[20] The narrator of the story, Carlos, has a tall tale to tell and his relatives come to the conclusion that he must be a liar since it is known that he published a story. " 'You see?' a cousin of mine who was cross-eyed said. 'That little guy's a liar. Look what he has written on this paper. A fibber from head to foot. Capable of inventing things no one knows anything about' " (p. 384).

Carlos tells of eight encounters he has with a man, Antón Luna, who claims to be his uncle. The meetings occur between 1911 and 1931 as the young boy is growing up, and since the uncle in question is supposedly dead, his appearance provokes a great deal of speculation and consternation among Carlos's relatives. It is even suggested that the man may be the boy's father, a claim which Carlos does not accept, and an issue which is never resolved in the story. Antón seeks the boy out during their first encounters and each brief visit is accompanied by a gift of money. Antón's monetary presents increase, then gradually decrease in size, and the last time Carlos sees him Antón is begging for handouts so he can indulge in drink. The narrator finally realizes that his visitor's financial state reflects the economic conditions of the country. "Whoever he was, that man was a monetary thermometer" (p. 386). In this regard, Antón is a mirror of the financial fortunes of a social order and his last name

"Luna" ("Moon") is suggestive of this role. Just as the moon's different phases are governed by the amount of light it receives from the sun, Antón's personal fortune is related to the economic conditions of society. Carlos carefully notes the different financial stages in the cycle of Antón's life and points out that he moves through periods of frugality, acquisition, speculation, and economic collapse. It is 1931 when Carlos last sees Antón; the inflationary period of the 1920s and the speculative orgy that accompanied it are over and the world is well into the Great Depression.

Carlos's last memory of Antón is the one that most vividly stands out in his mind, and it overshadows the positive connotations of the earlier meetings. "I've forgotten all the previous ones—the impressions of the good times. This is the one that stays with me. The man was walking, rigid, setting his feet firmly on the ground, and his sandals had the sound of those who beat the earth with rage. No, that man was not a ghost!" (p. 388). A puzzling story of gentle humor ends on a negative and skeptical note. However, Antón's decline into poverty has not crushed his spirit or his pride, and the narrator senses that his demeanor conveys a protest of his condition. Carlos's denial that Antón was a ghost underscores the lack of explanation of Antón's identity and the overwhelming reality of the social conditions of that time. The denial also reaffirms the narrator's unresolved doubts.

Carlos is a waif who lives with different relatives and there is no sense of permanence to his life. He is a burden to the many people who sometimes share the responsibility of caring for him, and, at times, Carlos complicates matters. Although he feigns innocence, he is responsible for the pregnancy of one of his Uncle Lorenzo's stepdaughters, an accomplishment that Antón and Lorenzo view with pride despite the outraged reactions of the girl's mother. It is not the only difficulty in which Carlos becomes involved. On another occasion he and another man come upon two girls bathing in a stream and Carlos explains: "What happened there, isn't for this story. The two of us had to mount up as fast as we could and escape, pursued by a band of men and dogs" (p. 383). Carlos acquires a reputation with women rivaled only by that of Antón, and the narrator is continually puzzled by Antón's knowledge of his escapades.

Antón is a source of protection and help to Carlos, although his visits are infrequent. Antón's unexpected appearances and the help he gives Carlos, when he has it to give, parallel the capricious and illogical nature of the narrator's life. Carlos had already noted the relationship between economic conditions and Antón's personal failure, and before his final encounter with Antón, he arrives at a number of other conclusions. Because five years have passed since he last saw Antón, Carlos had almost forgotten him, and he had become more preoccupied with the illogical nature of existence.

I had too much to think about at that time to rack my brains with his enigma. He wasn't the only mystery. Little by little things were accumulating in me for which I had no firm explanations, so that I ended up telling myself that I could only be sure of myself, and even then . . . What really intrigued me was what others were carrying inside them. One never knew what they would do or say the next day. Everything that was happening to me was induced by forces as illogical, as strange, as the apparitions of my Uncle Antón.

Perhaps because of that I tried to conform to the revolution that was building up. I needed to grasp something, believe in something, even though I didn't believe. (p. 387)

The mystery of Antón is unresolved in the story, for Antón is a metaphor of the capricious nature of the narrator's existence. Antón comes and goes, gives and takes, in a most unexpected and unexplained fashion and this parallels the type of life that the narrator leads. Antón's last appearance greatly impresses him because he is an incarnation of an existence that gives and takes in an erratic and illogical manner. The narrator's last impression of Antón endures because it represents perhaps the realization that those who provide are also subject to forces they do not control. The humor and wit of "Mi tío Antón Luna" help to create a tone that implies an acceptance and understanding of a difficult past, as well as a realization that individuals are not capable of giving more than they have. There is also a tinge of nostalgia in the story, and one can, if he wishes, assert that the author's declared intent in the introduction of "mixing reality in fantasy" has been successfully executed.[21] "Mi tío Antón Luna" constitutes a remarkable blend of fact and fiction that vitalizes and transforms memory.

IX *"La vaca en la azotea"*

"Un 'bum' " created ambivalence in the reader by the skillful manipulation of several polarities, and "Mi tío Antón Luna" leaves the identification of a major character unresolved to intensify the uncertainty the story conveys and to communicate the capricious nature of existence. "La vaca en la azotea" [The Cow on The Rooftop] of 1973 is a study in ambiguity—it represents a natural extension and development of an element present in some of the other stories of Novás Calvo's revolutionary period, as well as a refinement of a narrative mode he used so successfully in a story of the 1940s, "¡Trínquenme ahí a ese hombre!" The reader's perception of reality in both "La vaca en la azotea" and "¡Trínquenme ahí a ese hombre!" is confined to a single narrator's version of events, and there is no certainty he is being told the truth.

"The Cow on the Rooftop" begins by presenting an enigmatic title that seems to defy logic. The association of "cow" and "rooftop" appears strange and the reader's curiosity is immediately engaged. The seemingly illogical title is followed by the first lines in the story which are the opening of a letter: "My More than Forgotten Chucho Moquenque (wherever you may be)."[22] The contradiction found in the title of the story intensifies in this opening sentence. The reader asks how anyone can be more than forgotten and the indefinite location of Chucho only serves to increase the enigma. We have a specific element, a cow, located in a strange but definite place, and another entity, Chucho, indefinitely placed. In addition, Chucho's identity seems to be undergoing a process of denial in the narrator's mind. The title and opening line of this story introduce two procedures that form the narrative basis of the story. In the first instance, we have specific information that is strangely placed and this suggests a certain deformation or modification of reality. Secondly, a process of contradiction is contained in the first line which addresses and refers to a person as "More than Forgotten." The process involves the presentation of specific information which is immediately rejected. Reality, then, as perceived by the narrator, becomes either deformed or partially denied. The reader soon realizes that the constant fluctuation between the manipulation and rejection of reality forms an important dynamic of the narrator's personality, and as the story proceeds the distinction between denial and manipulation becomes blurred in the mind of the narrator.

"La vaca en la azotea" is presented in the form of a letter written by a woman, Rita Fernández, in an insane asylum. The letter is addressed to Chucho Moquenque, a man who abandoned her and their son thirteen years ago to the day of the letter, an indication of her obsession with this event. She plans to give the letter to her psychiatrist, Dr. Cabral, with whom she is having an affair, in the hopes he will forward it to Chucho; but since she speaks rather openly of her relations with her psychiatrist in the letter, this creates doubts as to her intentions. Rita's letter closes on a note of vacillation and uncertainty, and in a momentary suspension of her defense mechanisms she asks: "My doubt, Chucho, is this: Does Dr. Cabral really think I'm crazy? A thousand times I ask myself this question" (p. 116). Her qualms only increase the uncertainty in the mind of the reader about the true course of events.

Rita's letter concentrates on a narration of the unusual episodes in her life since Chucho abandoned her, but it also contains a summary of important incidents prior to his departure. What emerges is her hatred of the man who has so seriously hurt her, and the multiplicities of a complex woman. Although Rita's ironic salutation indicates that Chucho Moquenque is no longer remembered, he, of course, is not forgotten for he is a continual presence in her mind and an obsession that finally drives her to an incredible act of violence. Rita tells of being an actress in her youth and of her ability in daily life to play different roles to manipulate people. Her acting evidently was so successful that it created doubts in Chucho: "You remember, Chucho, that you always called me a born actress, perhaps because during those first years at the University I took part in some plays. What impressed you most was my role as a madwoman in the work by Novás Calvo. You told me then: 'But Rita, I'll bet you're really crazy. Impossible to pretend so well' " (p. 112). Evidently, from what Rita states, Chucho was never convinced of her love and was fearful that it was all an act. Chucho abandoned Rita when the Revolution broke out and he left Cuba, but we never know whether, as she suggests, he is a cynic who knows how to survive or if he took advantage of the situation to escape from personal as well as political difficulties. The motivation is really unimportant, for what is crucial is her hatred which eventually finds ample expression.

Rita struggles to survive the difficulties of living under a revolutionary government, and her son, Raulín, is taken from her and is raised by a special cadre. Although she laments his loss, she continues to survive and even acquires a cow which she keeps on the roof of her house. Her attachment to the animal becomes abnormal, an indication of her will to survive and her distortion of reality. "I've had some men in my life. I once loved you dearly, Chucho Moquenque. But I never loved anyone like I loved that cow" (p. 114). When Raulín unexpectedly returns after many years, he is a young man and he tells her that her obligation is to share her possessions with others. Rita's hatred of Chucho emerges and focuses on their son whom she regards as an incarnation of Chucho, and her animosity drives her to kill Raulín. The contrast between Rita's description of her son ("those sharp murderous teeth," "rat-like eyes," "cruel smile") and the fairly innocuous statements he makes ("Mom, it's wrong what you're doing. It's against the law. That cow has to be turned over to the people" p. 115) convey the intensity of her feelings and her sense of outrage at the double loss of Chucho and their son. Rita claims to have taken the part of a madwoman after shooting Raulín to avoid prosecution, but the reader doubts the accuracy of her assertion.

No, the shouts weren't mine anymore, they belonged to the other me, the actress, who now took my place for good. Because the one who was your Rita ceased to exist right there, and it was the other one who replaced her.

Within an hour the news was on the radio. The actress went fluttering around the house like a wounded bird. At times she sang, at times she laughed. She sank into long silences and then spoke with those no longer there. When the militia came she was doing ballet steps around her dead son, your murdered son, you yourself. (p. 115)

Rita's desperate attempts to exteriorize her guilt are conveyed by her identification of the actress as the cause of her violent acts and her continual references to her in the third person, as if the actress were really another person. Her confusion of her son with Chucho is also apparent in her identification of the two men as one entity.

"La vaca en la azotea" is a masterful creation that keeps the reader uncertain as to the veracity of Rita's version of events, and this ambiguity is central to the experience of the story. The reader's doubts parallel those of the deranged Rita who has difficulty distinguishing between the real and unreal. Rita's emotional confusion is conveyed to the reader and he finds himself an active participant in the nebulous world of Rita Fernández, trying, as she does, to find his way through the twisted labyrinth of her mind. What emerges from her narrative is the portrait of a person who has lost control of interior and exterior forces—she can no longer master her own emotions and actions, nor is she able to contain the direction taken by the social order that surrounds her. She is adrift and out of control and her crazy monologue parallels the turbulent course of the Revolution. Novás Calvo has captured in this story the emotional essence of an individual who is completely overwhelmed by exterior and interior forces.

X *"Hacia donde se acuesta el sol"* and *"En CopeyAbajo"*

The 1968–1973 period of Novás Calvo's writings is a particularly rewarding interval for it contains the most outstanding pieces of his revolutionary period. "Mi tío Antón Luna" and "La vaca en la azotea" represent a blending of the finest elements of Novás Calvo's art and combine new and early features of his work. The year 1973 also marked the appearance of "Hacia donde se acuesta el sol" ("Toward the Setting Sun"), a story which uses thematic and technical devices similar to those employed in "La vaca en la azotea." In both works a narrator directs his thoughts to an individual whose actions have had a major influence on the narrator's life, and in the two stories the person addressed is essentially absent. In "La vaca en la azotea" Rita Fernández directs her letter to Chucho Moquenque whom she has not seen in thirteen years and whose whereabouts are unknown to her. In "Hacia donde se acuesta el sol" the narrator, Guango López, centers his monologue on Fela Ramírez who is physically present, but Guango is unaware that she has died. They are adrift at sea and Guango is so delirious he does not recognize that Fela is dead. As the reader proceeds through each story, he begins to realize that the separation caused by distance or death contributes to a sense of isolation which permeates both works. The intensity of each narrator's emotional involvement with the person who is not present accentuates a feeling of isolation. Their monologues are colored by an obsessive frenzy that rages against the indifference that characterized Chucho's and Fela's attitudes toward them. Their anger contrasts vividly with the unconcern that victimized them. On the one hand, a definitive physical separation marks the nature of both relationships, but, on the other, Rita and Chucho never have disengaged emotionally from the individuals who dominate their thoughts. These contradictory tendencies heighten the tragedy of the stories.

Another similarity that both works share is that the narrators in "La vaca en la azotea" and "Hacia donde se acuesta el sol" are disoriented and have essentially lost their way. Rita is adrift in the labyrinths of madness, and Guango is delirious from physical exhaustion and is well on the road to death. The works portray different kinds of mental disintegration, one brought on by the denial and distortion of reality characteristic of mental illness, and the other the rambling thoughts of a man suffering from the physical and emotional deterioration caused by the hardships of being adrift at sea in a small boat. In a figurative and literal sense they are human flotsam, the debris of tangled and tortuous relationships. Although both narrators do not fully register the significance of all of their own observations, the reader becomes increasingly aware of the tragedy of their desperate situations. To a certain extent, Rita and Guango struggle to avoid recognizing the full implications of their hopeless state—Rita attempts to conceal her madness from herself and Guango suppresses the realization that his situation is futile and that he will soon die. The setting sun referred to in the title of "Hacia donde se acuesta el sol" is a metaphor of his fate. The two stories are fine examples of a predominant tendency in the works of Lino Novás Calvo, the attempts of many of his characters to blot out objective truth.

In "Hacia donde se acuesta el sol" Guango and Rita are attempting to escape from Cuba and as the story opens they are adrift in a rowboat. Guango reviews their past and dwells on his hopes that they will either reach the United States or be rescued. As Guango speaks to his dead companion he is not aware that their small boat is being swept into the Gulf of Mexico by an imperceptible but inexorable current. Caught in the grip of the silent stream, the boat appears to be as motionless as the nearly delirious narrator, and the easy flow of the narration matches the boat's unseen movement out to sea. "Hacia donde se acuesta el sol" is a story of a consciousness merging with death, and the fluidity of the style parallels the boat's journey into the formless mass of the sea. The work narrates acts of desperation born of despair and life's inevitable journey toward extinction. This story appeared in December 1973 at approximately the time Novás Calvo suffered a stroke. It is unfortunate and tragic that this happened precisely when his narrative creations were once again reaching the standards of excellence established during the 1930s and 1940s.

At the time of this writing I know of one additional story by Novás Calvo that has not been published.[23] "En CopeyAbajo" [Down in Copey] deals with the gradual arrival of different stages of the Revolution in an isolated rural area. The simple peasants scarcely comprehend the significance of the events that slowly engulf them. Near the end of the story two men find themselves unwittingly constructing a wall that is used as the site of their execution. The military officer who directs the firing squad had once been a member of the rural militia during the dictatorship of Fulgencio Batista, but he is now a revolutionary. His name, Carmona, recalls Novás Calvo's near-execution during the Spanish Civil War. "En CopeyAbajo" is characterized by its direct narration and negative view of the Revolution. In this regard, the work is similar to the revolutionary stories of the 1961–1963 period. There is an animistic element in "CopeyAbajo" which is related to the superstitions of the rural area.

XI The Contributions of Novás Calvo

Novás Calvo and the novelist Alejo Carpentier are mainly responsible for the establishment of a modern tradition in Cuban prose fiction. They are the most innovative and creative talents of their generation, meticulous and dedicated craftsmen who moved Cuban fiction from regional to universal concerns. Everyday language achieves a creative dimension that transcends regionalistic peculiarities in Novás Calvo's works, and his language frequently creates a poetic and hypnotic effect that captivates his reader. This mode of expression has been used subsequently by other Spanish-American writers, particularly Juan Rulfo of Mexico. Novás Calvo also has distinguished himself by his knowledge of the literature of the United States and his introduction of writers such as William Faulkner to the Spanish-speaking world.

Novás Calvo's vision is essentially existential in that his main concern is how individuals respond to difficult circumstances. He once stated: "I consider life to be a brutal struggle. At times we deceive ourselves and we don't see life as it is."[24] His emphasis is on the perception or distortion of reality rather than on the deterministic elements of existence that naturalistic writers elected to stress. In his stories characters may be overwhelmed by circumstances they cannot control, but he accentuates the way they choose to respond to their difficulties. The victim of the torment of a gang of youths in "Un dedo encima," for example, resorts to violence in order to break out of the circle of fear that engulfs him, and he disappears, never to be seen again by those who hunted him. The protagonist of "La noche de Ramón Yendía" loses control of his emotions, particularly his sense of guilt, and unwittingly provokes the chase that results in his death. He fails in his attempts to resist the social and political chaos that is developing and he becomes an extension of the disorder that surrounds him. A similar circumstance occurs in "La visión de Tamaría" for the protagonist of that story overreacts to a particular situation and becomes the victim of his most outstanding ability, his enormous strength as a swimmer. Propelled by panic to swim aimlessly into the ocean, he becomes disoriented and finally sinks into the formlessness of the sea.

Disorientation and irrationality are key ingredients in the stories we have mentioned, and they are central concerns in many of the works Novás Calvo has written. In some instances, the disorientation is predominantly psychological as in the case of "La vaca en la azotea" in which a woman in a mental hospital begins to wonder if her ability to act and fool others is feigned or real. This ambiguity in the mind of the narrator conveys very well the sense of psychological disintegration the story creates.

Social and psychic dissolution is another important aspect of Novás Calvo's works. It is an element in the stories we have discussed above and in works such as "La luna de los ñáñigos" ("En las afueras") and "Hacia donde se acuesta el sol." In the first-mentioned story an entire community falls victim to superstition and persecutes those upon whom it projects its fears, but, ultimately, in a fine example of ironic reversal, it becomes the victim of its own terrors and prejudices. Because of the community's collective actions, it simply ceases to exist. "Hacia donde se acuesta el sol" portrays the psychology of a mind merging with the ultimate dissolution—death. This topic is also masterfully presented in "Cayo Canas" in which the image of an enclosing circle is used to convey the impending and unavoidable disintegration of death.

The response to adverse circumstances, however, is not always necessarily tragic except, perhaps, in a moral sense. In "Mí tío Antón Luna" and "Hombre malo," for example, a fine sense of wit is incorporated into sections of the story, and the protagonist of "Hombre malo" escapes an unsavory situation by becoming a rogue. He is almost destroyed by an overdeveloped sense of responsibility, but he finally avoids this moral trap by embracing evil ways. Social conditions often have a warping effect in Novás Calvo's stories, and occasionally a character responds by rejecting morality as in *El negrero*. These topics reflect Novás Calvo's interest in those who rebel against moral and social norms.

Novás Calvo combines the thematic concerns we have commented upon with highly imaginative narrative modes. His narrators are weavers of tales and illusions and they often present a world not subject to rational control. In this regard, his stories are character-centered, in the sense that his characters' perceptions of reality are more important than the exterior world. In this respect, Novás Calvo's works are mind- or emotion-oriented and make no attempt to capture fully an objective, exterior reality. This procedure is well exemplified by the world created by the blind protagonist of "La visión de Tamaría." Indeed, his attempts to exteriorize his emotions in his love for a girl prove to be his undoing. Because of this particular emphasis on the individual, time frequently is a subjective entity as susceptible to the distortions or manipulations of the mind as any other aspect of reality. These modifications are sometimes conveyed by skillful verbal manipulations that create an aura of timelessness. This is particularly evident in stories such as "En el cayo" and "Un dedo encima."

Many of Novás Calvo's works concern individuals involved in a conflict between their own interior emotional being and the exterior world of material reality. "El hombre-araña," for example, portrays a man unable to accept the enormous changes a social revolution has made in his life, and this conflict is expressed by strange visions. Some of Novás Calvo's stories seem to imply that the achievement of an equilibrium between the interior world of the individual and the exterior world of reality can result in a perversion of the human spirit. The narrator of "Nadie a quien matar," for example, achieves such a balance but at the price of deceiving someone with whom he had always been close. The protagonist of "Hombre malo" becomes a success, but in order to achieve this end he abandons any sense of moral conscience.

Many of Novás Calvo's stories create an aura of mystery and a sense of dread of irrational forces, and his works convey the emotional disorientation that his characters experience. They respond in diverse ways in attempting to control their lives. Some endeavor to blot out objective truth and embrace self-deception or illusion, others try to separate themselves from a reality that is too difficult to accept, and some resort to violence. Their frantic efforts can result in their being the victims of their own destructive forces. The configuration of an enclosing circle is used in some stories to convey the inner tensions of such characters, or a work may center on a hunt or chase that has ritualistic overtones. However, human will and imagination occasionally triumph over adversity, for defeatism is not a salient characteristic of his protagonists. Novás Calvo's works suggest that an admirable quality of the human spirit can be found in the individual's capacity to struggle against enormous odds, and it is this unwillingness to bow to adversity that enables his characters to transcend the tragedy of their personal defeats.

Although he has not confined himself to any single narrative mode, Novás Calvo has demonstrated a preference for narration in the first-person singular throughout his career. The Argentine critic and writer Enrique Anderson-Imbert has pointed out that even when the narrator's position is external to the narrative action and third-person pronouns are used, the reader senses the presence of an "I."[25] This sensation is created in many instances by the narrator's presentation of events as seen by the characters. That is, the storyteller relates his tale, but events are presented as the characters perceive them. In addition, at times a narrator is split into two entities, the storyteller we listen to and a character within the work, and this relationship or division is not always obvious.

Novás Calvo frequently uses a language patterned on the rhythms and nuances of everyday speech. His narrator's view is retrospective in many stories, and as the speaker looks back and recounts events, the past becomes an actual present for the reader. This dual point of view is combined at times with a binary structuring of plot or the incorporation of a number of polarities within the text. These dualities create a sense of ambivalence or uncertainty in the reader and intensify the emotional tone of Novás's stories. Novás Calvo creates illusion and ambivalence by a stylistic blending of the specific and nonspecific, a technique that can be heightened by the use of irony. Some of his most successful creations terminate with an ironic reversal of events which surprises the reader or contradicts his expectations. Although his stories are characterized by their serious content, a fine sense of humor and wit enhance many works. The unwary reader may also find himself victimized by congenial but unreliable narrators.

Many of Novás Calvo's works concern individuals who are essentially outsiders and who are haunted by a vague uneasiness that they do not belong, an echo, perhaps, of the many vicissitudes of a difficult life. The series of emotional upheavals that interrupted the continuity of Novás Calvo's life undoubtedly sharpened his vision, enabling him to see the unusual in the common and the universal in the unique. However, in the final analysis, it is his creative ability that distinguishes his works, for the autobiographical, when it is present, is a point of departure rather than a goal. If there is one element that unifies most of his work in this respect, it is the realization that a sense of restlessness and incompleteness characterizes the contemporary human spirit. One can also say that his stories reflect an intuitive recognition that all human creations are imperfect and that no group has ever been able to create a social unit that successfully incorporates everyone. This is one of the ultimate tragedies of the human condition and a constant preoccupation of Novás's work. One can see manifestations of these concerns, for example, in "La luna de los ñáñingos" (1932), "Un dedo encima" (1942), and "La vaca en la azotea" (1973). It is ironic, but not unfitting, considering the repetitive patterns in his life, that Novás Calvo should close his career in exile, removed again from a sense of roots, an emotional orphan on an eternal pilgrimage.

Notes and References

Preface

1. "Lo que le llamaba la atención era que ni mi tono ni mi figura conjugaban con lo que sabía de mí: que—como él—había sido corresponsal de guerra, que—como él—había escrito cuentos de lucha y muerte, que—como él—había estado en el lugar de los hechos. Esto no rimaba con la persona que tenía delante. No podía haber mayor contraste: él era grande y fuerte; yo, pequeño y endeble; su voz era recia y dura; la mía débil y blanda; él era brusco y altanero; yo, cauteloso y humilde. Otra paradoja; Hemingway se parecía a su obra; yo no me parecía a la mía." "Adiós a Hemingway," *Bohemia Libre* 53, no. 41 (16 de julio de 1961): 50.

Chapter One

1. For more biographical information see Salvador Bueno, "Semblanza biográfica y crítica de un narrador," in *Medio siglo de literatura cubana* (La Habana, 1953), pp. 211–34, and Alberto Gutiérrez de la Solana, *Maneras de narrar: contraste de Lino Novás Calvo y Alfonso Hernández Catá* (New York, 1972).
2. Bueno, p. 216.
3. "En 1926 pasé ocho meses en Nueva York, donde entré también de contrabando, para regresar a La Habana con más rasguños que dólares." In introduction to *Un experimento en el Barrio Chino* (Madrid, 1936), p. 3.
4. Lino Novás Calvo, "Cuba literaria," *Gaceta Literaria* 5, no. 116 (15 de octubre de 1931): 9.
5. "Un día los mandé un poema proletario, el primero de este tipo que publicaron, y me dieron la mayor alegría de mi vida," "Cuba literaria," p. 9.
6. "Ibamos allí a las juntas de la *Revista de Avance*, y ellos todos hablaban de los escritores de vanguardia de Europa y América, y yo oía y callaba. A veces, venían escritores de Méjico y del Perú y de otras naciones. Me parecía que nada iba conmigo y que yo no podía meterme a hablar de lo que no podía entender bien, yo, un chófer. Muchos creían que yo era el que limpiaba las oficinas y no me hacían caso. Luego nos despedíamos en el parque San Juan de Dios, y yo iba, luego, por la noche, al café El Yauco a hablar con las apristas y comunistas que se reunían allí. Estos hablaron mal de los que dirigían la revista. Decían que representaban a la burguesía y que toda burguesía estaba podrida. A mí mismo me atacaban porque era

amigo de ellos, a pesar de mis poemas proletarios." In "Cuba literaria II," *Gaceta Literaria* 5, no. 118 (15 de noviembre de 1931): 1.

7. Interview with the author, June 8, 1962, New York City.

8. A detailed analysis of these poems is contained in the author's "Lino Novás Calvo and. the 'Revista de Avance,' " *Journal of Inter-American Studies* 10, no. 2 (April, 1968): 232–43.

9. *Revista de Avance* 3, no. 26 (15 de septiembre de 1928): 235. A complete listing of the publications of this journal is contained in Carlos Ripoll's *Indice de la Revista de Avance*, New York: 1969. For interpretative essays on the journal see Félix Lizaro, "La Revista de Avance," *Boletín de la Academia Cubana de la Lengua* 10, nos. 3 and 4 (julio-diciembre, 1961): 19–43, and Carlos Ripoll, " 'La Revista de Avance' (1927–30) vocero de vanguardismo y pórtico de revolución," *Revista Iberoamericana* 30, no. 58 (julio-diciembre, 1964): 261–82.

10. "El camarada," *Revista de Avance* 2, no. 21 (15 de abril de 1928): 8; "Proletario" 4, no. 23 (15 de junio de 1928): 146. Novás Calvo has stated that his first poem was inspired by a reading of Gorki. "Duda y resolución en Gorki," *Repertorio Americano* 32, no. 14 (17 de octubre de 1936): 1. Also in *Universidad* (México) 2, no. 10 (noviembre, 1936): 45.

11. "Miedo," *Revista de Avance* 4, no. 32 (15 de marzo de 1929): 78.

12. "D. Ramón tiene la pereza grande de los dioses paganos . . . que esperan la ofrenda de una vestial en quien vengar la ofensa del tiempo." "Un hombre arruinado," *Revista de Avance* 4, no. 32 (15 de marzo de 1929): 78.

13. "El ahogao," *Revista de Avance* 5, no. 44 (15 de mayo de 1930): 76, 81; "Vida y muerte de Pablo Triste," *Social* 15, no. 9 (septiembre, 1930): 51, 106.

14. "El blanco de sus ojos era cada día más blanco, y la sábana blanca que iba envolviendo su vida interior se traslucía al través de su piel. Si la vida pudiera continuar después de la muerte, llegaría un día en que su piel sería blanca, por contagio de la muerte blanca." "El flautista," *Social* 14, no. 7 (julio, 1931): 36.

15. "Un horror indescriptible hacia la vida." "La cabeza pensante," *Orbe* 1, no. 11 (22 de mayo de 1931): 25.

16. "Casi nadie en la ciudad conocía a Jacobo por aquel tiempo. Era distinto a los demás hombres, era un hombre raro a quien nadie conocía, de quien nadie se acordaba. Lo que había en él que las gentes no recordaban, que no apeleaba a la mente de las gentes, yo no lo sé." "La cabeza pensante," p. 25.

17. "Un encuentro singular," *Gaceta Literaria* 5, no. 113 (1 de septiembre de 1931): 6. Also available in *Maneras de contar* (New York, 1970).

18. Editorial statement, *Revista de la Habana* 1, nos. 7 and 9 (julio-agosto, 1930): v.

19. "Tenía entonces unos veinte años, y hacía cinco que recorría la Isla, trabajando aquí, vagando allá, siempre deseoso de dejar una faena para

emprender otra, y siempre con los bolsillos vacíos. Nunca había tenido grandes tropiezos, sin embargo. Mi timidez natural—no puedo afirmar que esté muy curado todavía,—me mandaba apartarme de riesgosas aventuras, y toda mi vida había sido un continuo moverse lentamente bajo el sol mientras que la fantasía me traía regalos inaprehendibles." "El bejuco," *Social* 16, no. 21 (diciembre, 1931): 27.

20. "La luna se levantaba sobre el cañaveral y lo doraba a plomo. A distancia se sentía el tambor de un barracón, donde los negros celebraban algún rito. Era un batir lúgubre y solemne. Un lamento fúnebre de cueros vivientes que se ahogaba en la calma sofocante de la noche." "El bejuco," p. 27.

21. "Su figura tenía todas las apariencias que debieron caracterizar a los primitivos inhabitantes de Cuba." "El bejuco," p. 28.

22. "Pero la tierra es vengativa." "El bejuco," pp. 28, 64.

23. "En el horizonte había desaparecido la línea divisoria entre el cielo y la tierra, y las estrellas se fundían en aquel espejismo total." "El bejuco," p. 64.

24. "Yo también nací en esta tierra, como tú; y como tú huí de la casa de mis padres para ser libre." "El bejuco," p. 28.

25. "Aquella locura, en la quietud espectral del campo, era lo que me fascinaba. La sentía invadirme, trepar por mis nervios y cuajarse en mis ojos. Era su aliento, de una peste densa, era la calavera de su rostro y los ojos sin pestañas, redondos, los que me apresaban. Era como una fuerza hipnótica, no viva, sino emanada de la tierra podrida, como si el campo fuera un inmenso cementerio y nosotros los únicos vivos." "El bejuco," p. 65.

26. "El Hombre estaba allí, a la margen del arroyo. Su cuerpo, caído, derribado sobre sí mismo, era ya una masa informe. La cabeza le colgaba sobre el agua, como si su último deseo fuera mirarse en aquel espejo. Sólo las manos—¡aquellos manos!—se estiraban hacia la tierra, enroscándose como serpientes a lo que pudo ser mi garganta—a aquello que fué el último asidero de su instincto: el tallo de un bejuco." "El bejuco," p. 65.

27. This writer once asked Novás Calvo which story had been awarded the prize by the *Revista de la Habana* and he wrote: "I don't remember it. It must have been of little value. I forgot it like so many others." ("El premiado por la *Revista de la Habana* no lo recuerdo. Debe haber sido poca cosa. Lo olvidé como tantos otros.") Letter to the author dated July 2, 1962. Actually, all of his stories published prior to 1932 except "Un hombre arruinado" have been neglected by critics and author. A close friend of Novás Calvo once remarked to me in a perceptive comment that Novás Calvo's life was like that of an orphan and his stories were his orphans. He turned them out into the world to fend for themselves.

28. "*Social* no era una revista literaria pero reflejaría, a veces sin proponérselo, todos los altibajos de nuestra vida cultural entre 1916 y 1930."

Ambrosio Fornet, *Antología del cuento cubano contemporáneo* (México, 1967), p. 20.

29. "En mi vida de emigrante, guardo esos preciosos regalos como consuelo de aquella, ya perdida para siempre—vida de aldea." In Arnold Chapman, *The Spanish American Reception of United States Fiction (1920–1940)* (Berkeley and Los Angeles, 1966), p. 175.

30. Ibid., p. 177.

31. Ibid., p. 178.

32. The two articles are "Quemando gasolina, confesiones de un 'botero,' " *Orbe* 1, no. 12 (29 de mayo de 1931): 14–15, and "¡Arre! mula, confesiones de un carrero," *Orbe* 1, no. 15 (19 de junio de 1931): 12–13.

33. Interview, June 8, 1962.

Chapter Two

1. This anecdote was related to me by Mrs. Novás Calvo in a telephone conversation in September, 1977. She reported that his mother stated: "A ti siempre te gustaba la manera de no trabajar."

2. Enrique Anderson-Imbert, "La originalidad de Lino Novás Calvo," *Symposium* 29, no. 3 (Fall, 1975): 212.

3. Interview, June 8, 1962.

4. "Su cintura se ponía en tensión como un cuero." "La luna de los ñáñigos," *Revista de Occidente* 10, no. 103 (enero, 1932): 93. The title of this story was changed to "En las afueras" when it appeared in *La luna nona* (Buenos Aires, 1942). Since our analysis is based on the original text and *La luna nona* is not easily available, the original Spanish will be included in the footnotes.

5. "Todos los sentidos se habían cerrado en ella para contener el secreto de la noche de la luna, y el bongó sonó desde entonces distincto, como si en su centro hubiera una luna muda, una luna de trapo." "La luna de los ñáñigos," pp. 89–90.

6. "Los cueros comenzaron a mugir como si su voz viniera de una selva muy lejana, como si no fuera más que el rumor muy distante de una selva de fieras." "La luna," p. 103.

7. "Puede que su sentido se expresara en música, en el cuero del bongó, una noche de luna, si hubiera en nuestros oídos algo con que engrampar el sentido de la música." "La luna," p. 83.

8. "Yo no sé por qué, pero había algo en aquel cuento que no quería salir todo junto y se iba a los ojos." "La luna," p. 86.

9. "Mi hija se dió candela porque era negra y porque tenía un blanco metido en la cabeza. Mi hija, Rita, era negra como el carbón y el hombre que tenía en la cabeza era blanco como la luz. Por eso mi hija se volvió contra su piel y la quemó. Mi hija está ahora en el infierno de los negros ardiendo hasta que llegue allí un blanco que tiene que ir a darle su piel para que pueda subir al cielo de los blancos." "La luna," p. 87.

10. "Sólo sabíamos que la música encendía nuestra sangre y que nuestros músculos se movían solos. La hoguera nos calentaba y ablandaba nuestras piernas y nuestras cinturas, y los cueros a bramar como tormentas que nos agitaran. Ninguno veía sino el fuego y ninguno oía sino el rugido. Cualquier ruido que no fuera nuestro, el de los negros, lo hubiéramos oído. Nadie lo oyó, sin embargo. Nadie oyó ni vió a Garrida entre nosotros." "La luna," p. 104.

11. The policeman does not appear in the 1942 version of the story. Also, the participants sense Garrida's presence in the very "magic" they are directing against her and they finally recognize her after she joins them. "En las afueras," *La luna nona,* p. 190.

12. "Nadie debe acercarse a ese cementerio, junto al mar, ni ver la luna de los ñáñigos." "La luna," p. 105.

13. "En el cayo," *Revista de Occidente* 10, 107 (mayo, 1932): 241. All other quotations are noted in the text. This story is also available in *La luna nona* (1942), and under the title of "El otro cayo" in *Cayo Canas* (Buenos Aires, 1946), *El otro cayo* (México, 1959), and Ambrosio Fornet's *Antología del cuento cubano contemporáneo* (México, 1967).

14. José Antonio Portuondo, "Four Cuban Novelists," *Books Abroad* 18, no. 2 (Spring, 1944): 238.

15. Lorraine Ben-Ur, "Lino Novás Calvo: A Sense of the Preternatural," *Symposium* 29, no. 3 (Fall, 1975): 221.

16. "Aquella noche salieron los muertos," *Revista de Occidente* 10, no. 114 (diciembre, 1932): 285. All other quotations are noted in the text. This story is also available in *La luna nona* (1942) and *Maneras de contar*.

Chapter Three

1. Interview, June 8, 1962.

2. Lino Novás Calvo, "Cuba Literaria II," *Gaceta Literaria* 5, no. 118 (15 de noviembre de 1931): 2.

3. For more information on the novel in Cuba see the author's *Major Cuban Novelists: Innovation and Tradition* (Columbia and London, 1976).

4. *El negrero* (Madrid, 1933), pp. 7–8. Several editions of this novel have been published by Espasa-Calpe. All quotations will be from the 1933 edition and will be noted in the text.

5. These novels have been published in English and the titles are those used in the translations.

6. Interview, June 8, 1962.

7. Bueno, *Medio siglo de literatura cubana,* p. 220.

8. "Vivía muy mal en España y París donde vivía de traducciones. Vivía miserablemente." Interview, August 28, 1962.

9. "Era una mujer como de treinta y cinco años, el rostro marcado por un prematuro desgaste interior, los ojos, ahora lánguidos, de un verdor intenso." *Un experimento en el Barrio Chino* (Madrid, 1936), p. 8. This is

a very scarce book. I know of only one library in the United States that has a copy.

10. See Vernon A. Chamberlin, "Symbolic Green: A Time-Honored Characterizing Device in Spanish Literature," *Hispania* 51, no. 1 (March, 1968): 29–37.

11. "Todas las cosas tienen el mismo valor en sí mismas. Sólo cuando se las agita se transforman . . . Cuando se las combina y se las agita. Esa es la vida." *Un experimento,* p. 12.

12. "La vida es tan monótona, y se va, se va inexorablemente. Los segundos empujan a los segundos. Para darse uno cuenta de que vive, tiene que crear siempre situaciones nuevas, ¿no? Experimentar con la vida." *Un experimento,* p. 35.

13. "En la cámara del centro, las luces parecían padecer por el desgaste de una floja energía acumulada." *Un experimento,* p. 5.

14. "Una luna naciente y redonda había cubierto el mar con una fosforescencia fantasmal." *Un experimento,* p. 6.

15. "Seguidamente, un bulto negro a la luz irreal partió de proa y avanzó a trompicones, semejante a un enorme gorila herido. Detrás de él brotó al instante otra figura blanca ésta, sin detalles precisos, silenciosa y vaga. Se sintió el jadear de una respiración cortada; luego, la figura negra avanzó disparada por un muelle interior, la cabeza echada hacia atrás, los dientes desnudos contra la luna, en dirección a la puerta de la cámara.

"La figura blanca se movió tras él como una vela solicitada por un remolcador." *Un experimento,* p. 6.

16. "El estilo y la técnica son más bien policiales, en escenas, como secuencias cinematográficas." Novás Calvo in letter to the author dated July 29, 1962.

17. "Es raro, me respondí; hace años que no sueño, desde que me casé . . ." *Un experimento,* p. 49.

18. "No paró de gritar en una hora, hasta que se la llevaron los guardias, todavía gritando . . ." *Un experimento,* p. 53.

19. "El barrio entero empezaba a cobrar un color lívido, amoratado y sepulcral." *Un experimento,* p. 55.

20. "Jacinta Sanromán se sentaba, rígida y misteriosa, junto a su vigilante, con la mirada fría perdida en el horizonte, hacia el Oriente. Su experimento había terminado dejando tan sólo un poso amargo en el fondo de su alma, un abatimiento y una paralización desesperantes, que sólo rompería la conmoción de una nueva aventura." *Un experimento,* p. 58.

21. Bueno, p. 222.

22. Interview, June 8, 1962.

23.
>No lloran, Federico, que estallaron
>las cuerdas de tu Sur atormentado;
>y galopa, de fuga, amedrentado,
>el eco del fragor a que callaron.

> Las Gracias que tus versos despertaron
> y en libres resonancias han mimado,
> volviéndose al poeta asesinado,
> de piedra calcinada se tornaron.
>
> No llora, Federico, que enrojece,
> la entraña que en romances palpitara
> con ardor de cadera estremecida:
>
> por pueblo que tu verso se merece,
> impune tanta ofensa no quedara,
> si a este pueblo costara cada vida.

"Soneto a Federico García Lorca," *Repetorio Americano* 32, no. 17 (7 de noviembre de 1936): 269.

24. "En el entierro de Pablo de la Torriente," *Repetorio Americano* 36, no. 4 (23 de enero de 1937): 52–53.

25. "El milagro," *Bohemia Libre* 54, no. 83 (29 de abril de 1962): 8–11, and "Fernández al paredón," *Bohemia Libre* 54, no. 86 (27 de mayo de 1962): 10–13, 82, 95. Both stories are also available in *Maneras de contar*, 1970.

26. The works were entitled "San José," "La cuota," and "En la masía." Conversation with Novás Calvo and his wife, New York City, December 29, 1978.

27. "Lo que vi en la guerra española es como para estar vomitando por el resto de mi vida." Bueno, p. 223.

28. "Fue como un padre para mí, como un santo." Interview, June 8, 1962.

Chapter Four

1. " 'Allies' and 'Germans,' " trans., Harriet de Onís, in *From the Green Antilles, Writings of the Caribbean*, Barbara Howes, ed. (London: Souvenir Press, 1967), p. 246. All other quotations from this story will be noted in the text.

2. Ambrosio Fornet, *Antología del cuento cubano contemporáneo*, p. 38.

3. Ambrosio Fornet, *En blanco y negro* (La Habana, 1967), p. 86.

4. Andrés Iduarte, "Lino Novás Calvo, La luna nona y otros cuentos," *Revista Hispánica Moderna* 12, nos. 1 and 2 (enero-abril, 1946): 63.

5. Hoffman R. Hays, "Lino Novás Calvo, La luna nona," *Books Abroad* 17, no. 3 (Summer, 1943): 241.

6. *Maneras de contar*, p. 27.

7. Interview, June 8, 1962.

8. For a detailed presentation of these historic events see Chapter 52 of Hugh Thomas, *Cuba, The Pursuit of Freedom* (New York, 1971).

9. "The Dark Night of Ramón Yendía," trans., Raymond Sayers, in *Spanish Stories and Tales*, Harriet de Onís, ed. (New York, 1954), p. 155. Other quotations from this story will be noted in the text.

10. Lino Novás Calvo, "Un dedo encima," *Cayo Canas* (Buenos Aires and México, 1946), p. 114. Other quotations will be noted in the text.

11. "La moraleja es bien evidente: para sobrevivir en esta sociedad viciada hay que 'hacerse malo'. El mundo entonces no ofrece muchas posibilidades de perfeccionamiento moral . . ." José Rodríguez Feo, "Los cuentos cubanos de Lino Novás Calvo," *Orígenes* (invierno, 1946), p. 28.

12. Lino Novás Calvo, "Long Island," *La luna nona y otros cuentos* (Buenos Aires, 1942), p. 116. Other quotations will be noted in the text. This story is available also in *El otro cayo*.

13. Interview, June 8, 1962.

14. Ibid.

15. Ibid.

16. "En cuanto a que tu hijo no haga mal a nadie, yo tengo mis ideas. De aquí no mandan más que hombres buenos . . . y tontos. Les cortan las uñas y les arrancan los dientes; los castran y los amansan; y luego los mandan a que se defiendan entre los lobos. Por eso me quiero llevar yo a este antes que crezca." "La primera lección," *La luna nona*, pp. 204-5.

17. "Por primera vez se mostraba tímido, y con un irresistible deseo de huir, de esconderse, y de evitar los flujos de sentimiento, verdadero o convencional." "La primera lección," pp. 205-6.

18. "Canadio permaneció así como obsesionado, inclinado sobre el arzón, mirando hacia dentro. Estaba aun así cuando la forma blanca y espectral— al sol blanco y espectral—de la ambulancia que llegaba tarde, asomó, balanceándose sobre el empedrado, sin campanilla, sin ruido de motor, como planeando, en lo alto del camino." "La luna nona," *La luna nona*, p. 43.

19. For a study of the influence of William Faulkner on Novás Calvo, see James E. Irby, *La influencia de William Faulkner en cuatro narradores hispanoamericanos* (Mexico City, 1956).

20. Fornet, *Antología del cuento cubano moderno*, p. 38

Chapter Five

1. The literal translation of *En los traspatios* is *In the Backyards*. I have used a title which, although different, more accurately reflects the content of the story.

2. See Salvador Bueno, *Medio siglo de literatura cubana*, pp. 232-34, and José Antonio Portuondo, "Lino Novás Calvo y el cuento hispanoamericano," in *El heroísmo intelectual* (Mexico, 1955), p. 51.

3. Fernando Ortiz, *El huracán, su mitología y sus símbolos* (México, 1947), pp. 72-73.

4. "El otro cayo" appeared under the title "En el cayo" in the *Revista de Occidente* in 1932 and in *La luna nona* (1942).
5. "La visión de Tamaría," *Cayo Canas*, p. 71. Also available in Salvador Bueno's *Antología del cuento en Cuba (1902–1952)* (La Habana, 1953).
6. "Cayo Canas," *Cayo Canas*, p. 9.
7. "No le sé desil," *Cayo Canas*, p. 121.
8. "¡Trínquenme ahí a ese hombre!" *Cayo Canas*, p. 132.
9. "Camilia Timiraos cuenta," *Cuadernos Americanos* 35, no. 5 (septiembre–octubre, 1947): 264–81, and "Esto también es gritar," *Cuadernos Americanos* (julio–agosto, 1948), pp. 261–82.
10. "El cuarto de morir," *Orígenes* 5, no. 18 (verano, 1948): 3–13, and "A ese lugar donde me llaman," *Orígenes* 8, no. 27 (1951): 18–24.
11. "A ese lugar donde me llaman," *Maneras de contar* (New York, 1970), p. 63.
12. An example of this type of journalistic writing is "Elsa Colina y los tantos millones," *Bohemia* (31 de agosto de 1953), pp. 4–6, 8, 129–31, 137–39.
13. "La estructura de la novela policíaca es la más bien hecha." Interview, June 8, 1962.
14. Salvador Bueno, *Medio siglo de literatura cubana*, pp. 225–27.
15. Interview, June 8, 1962.
16. Lino Novás Calvo, "Adiós a Hemingway," *Bohemia Libre* 53, no. 41 (16 de julio de 1961): 50.

Chapter Six

1. *Boletín Cultural*, Ministerio de Relaciones Exteriores de la República de Cuba, 1, no. 3 (febrero, 1960): 10.
2. Interview, June 8, 1962.
3. Novás Calvo told me in a bemused fashion that "Con un nudo en el corazón" was originally written for *Vanidades*, the magazine his wife edited. However, she thought it was too harsh for a women's journal and declined to publish it. Interview, June 8, 1962.
4. The stories that appeared in *Bohemia Libre* in their chronological order of publication are: "Con un nudo en el corazón," 53, no. 64 (24 de diciembre de 1961); "Un buchito de café," 53, 65 (31 de diciembre de 1961); "El milagro," 54, 82 (29 de abril de 1962); "La abuela reina y el sobrino Delfín," 54, 92 (8 de julio de 1962); and "El hombre-araña," 54, 6 (12 de mayo de 1963). All of these stories except "Con un nudo en el corazón" were republished in *Maneras de contar*. Quotations from these stories will be cited from *Maneras de contar* since it is more readily accessible.
5. "Fernández al paredón," *Maneras de contar*, p. 171. Other quotations will be cited in the text.
6. "La abuela reina y el sobrino Delfín," *Maneras de contar*, p. 125. Other quotations will be in the text.

7. Seymour Menton, *Prose Fiction of the Cuban Revolution* (Austin and London, 1975), pp. 236–37.

8. "El hombre-araña," *Maneras de contar*, p. 304. Other quotations will be cited in the text.

9. J. E. Cirlot, *A Dictionary of Symbols*, trans. Jack Sage (New York: Philosophical Library, 1962), p. 290.

10. Matías Montes Huidobro's novel *Desterrados al fuego* (México: Fondo de Cultura Económica, 1975) deals with the psychological disintegration produced by exile.

11. Lino Novás Calvo, "Un 'bum,' " *Exilio* 1, no. 2 (invierno, 1965) and "La noche en que Juan tumbó a Pedro," *Revista de Occidente*, no. 30 (septiembre, 1965). Herminia del Portal has stated that Novás Calvo published some short stories anonymously in *Vanidades* in the early 1960s, but she was unable to locate them at the time of this writing.

12. *Maneras de contar*, p. 281.

13. The earlier stories in *Maneras de contar* are "Un encuentro singular" (1931); "Aquella noche salieron los muertos" (1933); "Long Island" and "La noche de Ramón Yendía" (1942); "A ese lugar donde me llaman" (1951).

14. The stories in their chronological order of appearance: "El secreto de Narciso Campana," *Papeles de Son Armadans*, no. 151 (octubre, 1960); "Una cita en Mayanima," *Exilio* 2, nos. 1 and 2 (primavera - verano, 1968); "Peor que un infierno," *Revista de Occidente*, no. 74 (mayo, 1969); "Mi tío Antón Luna," *Revista Nacional de Cultura* (diciembre, 1969); "El esposo invisible," *Maneras de contar* (1970); "Nadie a quien matar," *Maneras de contar* (1970); "La gripe española," *Papeles de Son Armadans*, no. 172 (mayo, 1971); "Crónica roja," *Exilio*, 7, no. 4 (invierno, 1973); "La vaca en la azotea," *Papeles de Son Armadans*, no. 204 (mayo, 1973); "Hacia donde se acuesta el sol," *Papeles de Son Armadans*, no. 213 (diciembre, 1973).

15. *Maneras de contar*, p. 7.

16. *Maneras de contar*, p. 9. Other quotations from "Peor que un infierno" will be from this edition and will be noted in the text.

17. *Maneras de contar*, p. 392. Other quotations from this story will be noted in the text.

18. The use of the name Cecilia Valdés seems typical of a process of reversal or negation utilized in this story. This character's name recalls a famous nineteenth-century Cuban novel of customs, *Cecilia Valdés* by Cirilo Villaverde. Villaverde's Cecilia occupies a social position exactly opposite to that of the woman in Novás Calvo's story.

19. *Maneras de contar*, p. 77. Further quotations will be noted in the text.

20. *Maneras de contar*, p. 387. Other quotations will be noted in the text.

21. *Maneras de contar*, p. 371.

22. "The Cow on the Rooftop," trans. Myron I. Lichtblau, *Latin American Literary Review* 4, no. 7 (Fall - Winter, 1975): 116. Other quotations will be from this translation and are noted in the text.

23. The manuscript is in the possession of Julio Hernández-Miyares who plans to publish it in a collection of short stories. Professor Hernández-Miyares generously provided me a copy of the story.

24. "La vida la considero una lucha brutal. A veces nos engañamos a nosotros mismos y no vemos la vida como es." Interview, June 8, 1962.

25. Enrique Anderson-Imbert, "La originalidad de Lino Novás Calvo," p. 217.

Selected Bibliography

PRIMARY SOURCES

1. Books

Cayo Canas. Buenos Aires: Espasa–Calpe, 1946. The following lists the contents and the original date of publication of works that had appeared previously: " 'Aliados' y 'Alemanes' " (1940), "Cayo Canas," "Un dedo encima," "El otro cayo" (as "En el cayo" in 1932), "No le sé desil," "¡Trínquenme ahí a ese hombre!" (1944), and "La visión de Tamaría."

Un experimento en el Barrio Chino. Madrid: Editores Reunidos, 1936. Published in the series *La novela de una hora* l, no. 15 (26 de junio de 1936).

La luna nona y otros cuentos. Buenos Aires: Ediciones Nuevo Romance, 1942. Contains: "Aquella noche salieron los muertos" (1932), "En las afueras" (as "La luna de los ñáñigos" in 1932), "Hombre malo," "Long Island," "La luna nona," "La noche de Ramón Yendía," and "La primera lección."

Maneras de contar. New York: Las Américas Publishing Co., 1970. Contains: "La abuela reina y el sobrino Delfín" (1962), "Aquella noche salieron los muertos" (1932), "Un buchito de café (1961), "Un 'bum' " (1965), "Una cita en Mayanima" (1968), "Un encuentro singular" (1931), "A ese lugar donde me llaman" (1951), "El esposo invisible," "Fernández al paredón" (1962), "El hombre-araña" (1963), "Long Island" (1942), "El milagro" (1962), "Nadie a quien matar," "La noche de Ramón Yendía" (1942), "La noche en que Juan tumbó a Pedro" (1965), "Peor que un infierno" (1969), "El secreto de Narciso Campana" (1968), and "Mi tío Antón Luna" (1969).

El negrero. Madrid: Espasa-Calpe, 1933.

No sé quién soy. México: Colección Lunes, 1945.

El otro cayo. México: Ediciones Nuevo Mundo, 1959. Contains: "Cayo Canas," "Hombre malo" (1942), "Long Island" (1942), "No le sé desil" (1946), and "El otro cayo" (as "En el cayo" in 1932).

2. Periodicals

"La abuela reina y el sobrino Delfín." *Bohemia Libre* 54, no. 92 (8 de julio de 1962): 6–9, 80, 82–83. (short story)

"Adiós a Hemingway." *Bohemia Libre* 53, no. 41 (16 de julio de 1961): 50–51. (article)

"El adiós al 'barrio chino' barcelonés." *El Mundo Gráfico* (25 de mayo de 1936). (article)

"¿Adónde va nuestra narrativa?" *Exilio* 6, no. 3 (otoño, 1972): 21–26. (article)

"El ahogao." *Revista de Avance* 5, no. 44 (15 de marzo de 1930): 76–81. (play)
" 'Aliados' y 'alemanes.' " *Romance* 1, no. 17 (22 de octubre de 1940): 8, 14. (short story)
"¡Arre! mula, confesiones de un carrero." *Orbe* 1, no. 15 (19 de junio de 1931): 12–13. (article)
"Por la aldea de Galicia." *Orbe* 1, no. 24 (21 de agosto de 1931): 18–19. (article)
"Los ánimos literarios en Cuba." *Revista de Occidente* 41 (1933): 235–40. (article)
"Aquella noche salieron los muertos." *Revista de Occidente* 38, no. 114 (diciembre, 1932): 285–322. (short story)
"Así era William Faulkner." *Bohemia Libre* 54, no. 94 (22 julio de 1962): 54–55, 59. (article)
"El Ateneo de Madrid." *Orbe* 2, no. 48 (14 de febrero de 1932): 18–19. (article)
"Y baila y baila." *Bohemia* (22 de abril de 1951). (crime story)
"El bejuco." *Social* 16, no. 12 (diciembre, 1931): 27-28, 64–65. (short story)
" 'Buceando' en la tercera, de la Habana a Nueva York." *Orbe* 1, no. 20 (24 de julio de 1931): 18–19. (article)
"Un buchito de café." *Bohemia Libre* 53, no. 65 (31 de diciembre de 1961): 4–7, 94–95. (short story)
"Un 'bum.' " *Exilio* 1, no. 2 (invierno, 1965): 5–11. (short story)
"La cabeza pensante." *Orbe* 1, no. 11 (22 de mayo de 1931): 25. (short story)
"El camarada." *Revista de Avance* 2, no. 21 (15 de abril de 1928): 8. (poem)
"Camilia Timiraos cuenta." *Cuadernos Americanos* 35, no. 5 (septiembre-octubre, 1947): 264–81. (fragment of novel *Los Oquendo*)
"En el cayo." *Revista de Occidente* 36, no. 107 (mayo, 1932): 235–69. (short story)
"Los choferes." *Orbe* 1, no. 41 (25 de diciembre de 1931): 22–23. (article)
"En CopeyAbajo." Unpublished manuscript in possession of Julio Hernández-Miyares. (short story)
"Una cita en Mayanima." *Exilio* 2, nos. 1 and 2, (primavera-verano, 1968): 75–83. (short story)
"Crónica roja." *Exilio* 7, no. 4 (invierno, 1973): 95–102. (short story)
"El cuarto de morir." *Orígenes* 5, no. 18 (verano, 1948): 3–13. (short story)
"Cuba literaria." *Gaceta Literaria* 5, no. 116 (15 de octubre de 1931): 9–10. (article)
"Cuba literaria II." *Gaceta Literaria* 5, no. 118 (15 de noviembre de 1931): 1–4. (article)
"Los cuentos de Lydia Cabrera." *Exilio* 3, no. 2 (verano, 1969): 17–20. (article)
"Daisy Tornasol." *Revista de Avance* 4, no. 32 (15 de marzo de 1929): 77. (poem)

"Don Fernando. Su azúcar y su tabaco." *Repertorio Americano* 38, no. 2 (11 de enero de 1941): 25–26. (article)

"Don Ramón María del Valle-Inclán, Presidente del Ateneo." *Orbe* 2, no. 69 (3 de julio de 1932): 20. (article)

"Dos escritores americanos." *Revista de Occidente* 39 (1933): 92–98. (article)

"Duda y resolución en Gorki." *Repertorio Americano* 32, no. 14 (17 de octubre de 1936): 1–3. Also in *Universidad* 2, no. 10 (noviembre, 1936): 45–47. (article)

"Su ejemplo." *Revista de Avance* 5, no. 47 (15 de junio de 1930): 173–74. (article)

"Elsa Colina y los tantos millones." *Bohemia* (31 de agosto de 1952): 4–6, 8, 129–31, 137–39. (crime story)

"Un encuentro singular." *Gaceta Literaria* 5, no. 113 (1 de septiembre de 1931): 6–7. (short story)

"En el entierro de Pablo de la Torriente." *Repertorio Americano* 36, no. 4 (23 de enero de 1937): 51–52. (article)

"A ese lugar donde me llaman." *Orígenes* 8, no. 27 (1951): 18–24. (short story)

"El estilo que falta." *Boletín de la Academia Cubana de la Lengua* 1, no. 4 (octubre - diciembre, 1952): 620–23. (article)

Esto también es gritar." *Cuadernos Americanos* 7 (julio-agosto, 1948): 261–82. (fragment of novel *Los Oquendo*)

"Fernández al paredón." *Bohemia Libre* 54, no. 86 (27 de mayo de 1962): 10–13, 82, 95. (short story)

"El flautista." *Social* 14, no. 7 (julio, 1931): 36. (short story)

"El frente de los intelectuales, Ortega y Gasset, Marañón, Juan Ramón Jiménez, Bergamín, Adolfo Salazar y Guillermo de Torre hablan del movimiento." *El Mundo Gráfico* (2 de septiembre de 1936). (interview)

"Granitos de maíz." *Exilio* 6, no. 1 (primavera, 1972): 83–94. (short story)

"La gripe española." *Papeles de Son Armadans,* no. 182 (mayo, 1971): 179–88. (short story)

"Hacia donde se acuesta el sol." *Papeles de Son Armadans,* no. 213 (diciembre, 1973): 271–88. (short story)

"Hermana." *Revista de Avance* 4, no. 39 (15 de octubre de 1929): 305. (poem)

"Hermano." *Revista de Avance* 4, no. 32. (15 de marzo de 1929): 78. (poem)

"El hombre-araña." *Bohemia Libre* 54, no. 6 (12 de mayo de 1963): 7–8, 63. (short story)

"Un hombre arruinado." *Revista de Avance* 4, no. 40 (15 de noviembre de 1929): 335–36, 348. (short story)

"José María Chacón, el hombre." *Orbe* 1, no. 40 (18 de diciembre de 1931); 20–21. (article)

"José María Chacón, el peregrino de los archivos." *Repertorio Americano* 31, no. 16 (9 de abril de 1936): 249–50, 31 no. 17 (16 de abril de 1936), 260–62. (article)

"Lejanía." *Revista de Avance* 4, no. 32 (15 de marzo de 1929): 77. (poem)
"León Tolstoi." *Revista de Avance* 3, no. 26 (15 de septiembre de 1928): 242–43, 259. (article)
"La luna de los ñáñigos." *Revista de Occidente* 35, no. 103 (enero, 1932): 83–105. (short story)
"Manhattan Transfer, John Dos Passos." *Revista de Avance* 4, no. 39 (15 de octubre de 1929): 312. (review)
"Miedo." *Revista de Avance* 4, no. 32 (15 de marzo de 1929): 78. (poem)
"El milagro." *Bohemia Libre* 54, no. 82 (29 de abril de 1962): 8–11. (short story)
"Nena." *Revista de Avance* 4, no. 32 (15 de marzo de 1929); 77. (poem)
"La noche en que Juan tumbó a Pedro." *Revista de Occidente* 3, no. 30 (septiembre, 1965): 328–43. (short story)
"Novela por hacer." *Revista Bimestral Cubana* 47, no. 3 (mayo-junio, 1941): 348–59. (article)
"Con un nudo en el corazón." *Bohemia Libre* 53, no. 64 (24 de diciembre de 1961): 15, 67, 78. (short story)
"Panorama." *Revista de Avance* 3, no. 24 (15 de julio de 1928): 199. (poem)
"Un paseo por la Quinta Avenida." *Bohemia* (29 de julio de 1951). (crime story)
"El pathos cubano." *Homenaje a Enrique José Varona*. La Habana: Publicaciones de la Secretaría de Educación, 1935, 211–26. (article)
"Peor que un infierno." *Revista de Occidente*, no. 74 (mayo, 1969), 203–19. (short story)
"Proletario." *Revista de Avance* 3, no. 23 (15 de junio de 1928): 146. (poem)
"Quemando gasolina, confesiones de un carrero." *Orbe* 1, no. 12 (29 de mayo de 1931): 14–15. (article)
"El secreto de Narciso Campana." *Papeles de Son Armadans*, no. 151 (octubre, 1968), 39–76. (short story)
"Sobre ciegos y locos." *Exilio* 2, nos. 1 and 2 (primavera - verano, 1968): 119–21. (article)
"Soneto a Federico García Lorca." *Repertorio Americano* 32, no. 17 (7 de noviembre de 1936): 269. (poem)
"Mi tío Antón Luna." *Revista Nacional de Cultura*, Caracas (diciembre, 1969), 60–68. (short story)
"¡Trínquenme bien ahí a ese hombre!" *Orígenes* 1, no. 1 (primavera, 1944): 26–30. (short story)
"La vaca en la azotea." *Papeles de Son Armadans*, no. 204 (marzo, 1973), 281–92. (short story)
"Vida y muerte de Pablo Triste." *Social* 15, no. 9 (septiembre, 1930): 51, 106. (short story)

3. Translations

"'Allies' and 'Germans.'" Harriet de Onís, trans. In *From the Green Antilles, Writings of the Caribbean,* Barbara Howes, ed. Worchester and London: Souvenir Press, 1967, 244–56.

"As I Am . . . As I Was," Paul Bowles, trans. In *The Eye of the Heart,* Barbara Howes, ed. Indianapolis: Bobbs-Merrill Co., 1973, 159–68.

"The Cow on the Rooftop." Myron I. Lichtblau, trans., *Latin American Literary Review* 4, no. 7 (Fall-Winter, 1975): 109–16.

"The Dark Night of Ramón Yendía." Raymond Sayers, trans. In *Spanish Stories and Tales,* Harriet de Onís, ed. New York: Alfred A. Knopf, 1954, 139–64.

"That Night." In *Short Stories of Latin America,* Auturo Torres-Ríoseco, ed., New York: Las Américas Publishing Co., 1963, 25-54.

SECONDARY SOURCES

1. Books

BUENO, SALVADOR. *Antología del cuento en Cuba, 1902-1952*. La Habana: Dirección de Cultura del Ministerio de Educación, 1953. This anthology presents a useful panorama of the short story in Cuba during the first half of the twentieth century. Bueno divides Novás Calvo's works into two general categories—stories of adventure and of the subconscious. The anthology contains "La noche de Ramón Yendía" and "La visión de Tamaría." These are excellent stories, but they represent only one of the narrative modes utilized by Novás Calvo.

———. *Medio siglo de literatura cubana (1902–1952)*. La Habana: Publicaciones de la Comisión Nacional de Unesco, 1953. This volume contains an evaluation of Novás Calvo's works and is one of the basic sources of biographical information.

CHAPMAN, ARNOLD. *The Spanish American Reception of United States Fiction 1920–1940*. Berkeley and Los Angeles: University of California Press, 1966. A carefully researched study of the presence of U. S. fiction in Spanish America. The appendix includes two letters and a poem Novás Calvo sent Sherwood Anderson.

COLL, EDNA. *Indice informativo de la novela hispanaoamericana, Tomo I Las Antillas*. Universidad de Puerto Rico: Editorial Universitaria, 1974. An alphabetical listing of authors by country that includes biographical information, summaries of the contents of their works, and bibliographical listings of critical materials published in Spanish. Evaluative comments are included. This ambitious and useful work has been compiled by a researcher who is not overawed by contemporary experimental literature.

FORNET, AMBROSIO. *Antología del cuento cubano contemporáneo*. México: Ediciones Era, 1967. This anthology includes an informative and succint review of the development and evolution of Cuban prose fiction.

The author walks a tightrope between political and aesthetic considerations.

———. *En blanco y negro*. La Habana: Instituto del Libro, 1967. This book contains essentially the same essay listed in the previous entry. The commentary is followed by a valuable chronology of important national and international events, and significant publications that appeared in and outside of Cuba between 1900 and 1958.

GUTIERREZ DE LA SOLANA, ALBERTO. *Maneras de narrar: Contraste de Lino Novás Calvo y Alfonso Hernández Catá*. New York: Torres, 1972. A comparative study of the two mentioned writers with emphasis on biographical as well as aesthetic factors.

IRBY, JAMES EAST. *La influencia de William Faulkner en cuatro narradores hispanoamericanos*. México: n. p., 1956. This master's thesis is an early serious study of Novás Calvo's work.

JACKSON, RICHARD L. *The Black Image in Latin American Literature*. Albuquerque: University of New Mexico Press, 1976. This thematic and historical study singles out Novás Calvo's *El negrero* for its accurate treatment of the slave trade.

LEAL, LUIS. *Historia del cuento hispanoamericano*. México: Ediciones de Andrea, 1966. Contains a brief summary of Novás Calvo's importance and points out that "La noche de Ramón Yendía" anticipates Alejo Carpentier's *El acoso*.

MENTON, SEYMOUR. *El cuento hispanoamericano, 2*. México: Fondo de Cultura Económica, 1964. This anthology of short stories contains a brief analysis of "La noche de Ramón Yendía" which centers on the universal characteristics of the work.

———. *Prose Fiction of the Cuban Revolution*. Austin and London: University of Texas Press, 1975. This is the most complete study to date of the prose fiction of the revolutionary period, and it examines the relationships between politics and art. The section on Novás Calvo focuses on the influence of the Cuban Revolution on the stories Novás Calvo published between 1960 and 1970.

ORTIZ, FERANDO. *El huracán, su mitología y sus símbolos*. México: Fondo de Cultura Económica, 1947. Fernando Ortiz's anthropological and sociological studies have greatly influenced Cuban intellectual life. Of particular value is *Cuban Counterpoint: Tobacco and Sugar*, Harriet de Onís, trans. New York: A. A. Knopf, 1947.

PORTUONDO, JOSE ANTONIO. *El heroísmo intelectual*. México: Tezontle, 1955. This collection of previously published articles includes "Lino Novás Calvo y el cuento hispanoamericano" which appeared in *Cuadernos Americanos* 35, no. 5 (septiembre-octubre, 1947), 245–63. This critic and Salvador Bueno contributed greatly to the recognition of Novás Calvo in Spanish America. This essay places Novás Calvo's writings within the context of Spanish-American and Western fiction.

RIPOLL, CARLOS. *Indice de la Revista de Avance*. New York: Las Américas, 1969. An annotated listing of the contents of this important Cuban literary journal.

SOUZA, RAYMOND D. *Major Cuban Novelists: Innovation and Tradition*. Columbia and London: University of Missouri Press, 1976. The introductory chapter contains a comparison of the works of Alejo Carpentier and Novás Calvo.

THOMAS, HUGH. *Cuba, The Pursuit of Freedom*. New York: Harper and Row, 1971. A thorough and extensive history of Cuba.

2. Articles

ANDERSON-IMBERT, ENRIQUE. "La originalidad de Lino Novás Calvo." *Symposium* 29, no. 3 (Fall, 1975): 212-19. A valuable study that concentrates on the stories published in the *Revista de Occidente* in 1932. The author explains how these works were innovative, yet independent of the experimental tendencies of that period. The article also contains some general observations on the most salient characteristics of Novás Calvo's prose fiction.

BEN-UR, LORRAINE. "La época española de Novás Calvo: 1931-1939." *Chasqui* 6, no. 3 (mayo, 1977): 69-76. A survey of Novás Calvo's years in Spain and the influence of this period on his work. The article contends that Novás Calvo developed an authentic literary expression during this period.

———. "Lino Novás Calvo: A Sense of the Preternatural." *Symposium* 29, no. 3 (Fall, 1975): 220-28. A perceptive examination of "that which is strange and inexplicable but not miraculous" in the works of Novás Calvo. The article explains how supernatural elements are incorporated into certain stories without changing the natural order. The study concentrates on "La luna de los ñáñigos," "Aquella noche salieron los muertos," "La abuela reina y el sobrino Delfín," and "Mi tío Antón Luna."

BUENO, SALVADOR. "El cuento cubano contemporáneo." *El Hijo Pródigo* 4, no. 42 (septiembre, 1946): 141-47. A useful survey of the development of the short story in Cuba in the twentieth century. Four writers are selected for special treatment: Luis Felipe Rodríguez, Carlos Montenegro, Enrique Serpa, and Novás Calvo.

———. "Un cuentista cubano." *Américas* 3, no. 3 (marzo, 1951): 10-11, 41, 44-45. A general introduction to the works of Novás Calvo.

CLINTON, STEPHEN. "The Scapegoat Archetype as a Principle of Composition in Novás Calvo's 'Un dedo encima.'" *Hispania*, 62: 1 (March, 1979): 56-61. A very insightful study which sheds light on the narration, theme, and ending of the story analyzed.

FERNANDEZ, SERGIO. "Lino Novás Calvo, hechizador de negros." *Universidad*, nos. 14-15 (abril, 1957), 47-55. A fine analysis of "El otro

cayo" that studies the characters' attempts to escape from a monstrous reality.
FERRAN, JAIME. "Lino Novás Calvo." *Symposium* 29, no. 3 (Fall, 1975): 189–92. An introduction to a special issue of *Symposium* dedicated to Novás Calvo that presents some general observations on Novás Calvo's works and interesting comments on the man behind the stories.
GALBIS, IGNACIO R. M. "Tanatología en la narrativa de Novás Calvo." *Symposium* 29, no. 3 (Fall, 1975): 229–42. A survey of the manifestation of death in the works of Novás Calvo.
GARCIA VEGA, LORENZO. *Antología de la novela cubana.* La Habana: Dirección General de Cultura, Ministerio de Educación, 1960. This anthology covers the nineteenth and twentieth centuries and contains a selection from *El negrero.* Although it is very difficult to convey the essence of a novel in such a collection, the anthology does provide a fragmentary sampling of twenty-three authors. García Vega is more favorably inclined toward Novás Calvo's stories than his novel.
GUTIERREZ DE LA SOLANDA, ALBERTO. "Lino Novás Calvo: literatura y experiencia." *Caribe* 2, no. 1 (primavera, 1977): 61–75. A recent interview with Novás Calvo, and his wife, Herminia del Portal.
———. "Novás Calvo: precursor y renovador." *Symposium* 29, no. 3 (Fall, 1975): 243–54. A wide-ranging survey of Novás Calvo's career and literary significance.
HAYS, HOFFMAN R. "Lino Novás Calvo: 'La luna nona.'" *Books Abroad* 17, no. 3 (Summer, 1943): 241. An early review in English of Novás Calvo's most important book. Sees Novás Calvo as "a master of understatement and irony."
HOMS, ERNESTO. "Novás Calvo, su cachima y su cuchitril." *Orbe* 1, no. 36 (20 de noviembre de 1931): 12, 38. This interesting interview took place shortly after Novás Calvo's arrival in Spain in 1931. It reveals the young writer's views on art and his attachment and affection for Cuba.
LEAL, LUIS. "The Pursued Hero: 'La noche de Ramón Yendía.'" *Symposium* 29, no. 3 (Fall, 1975): 255–60. A study of the alienated hero figure in "La noche de Ramón Yendía," Ernest Hemingway's "The Killers," Jorge Luis Borges's "La espera," Alejo Carpentier's *El acoso*, Salvador Elizondo's "En la playa," and José Emilio Pacheco's *Morirás lejos*.
LICHTBLAU, MYRON I. "Reality and Unreality in 'La vaca en la azotea.'" *Symposium* 29, no. 3 (Fall, 1975): 261–65. An engaging analysis of the problem of narrative veracity in this particular story.
———. "Visión irónica en tres cuentos de Lino Novás Calvo." *Caribe* 1, no. 2 (otoño, 1976): 21–27. A study of the use of irony in "El esposo invisible," "Un 'bum,'" and "Hombre malo." The author views irony as a manifestation of Novás Calvo's recognition of the complexities of existence and the limitations of human knowledge.

LIZARO, FELIX. "La Revista de Avance." *Boletín de la Academia Cubana de la Lengua* 10, nos. 3–4 (julio-diciembre, 1961): 19–43. Originally presented as a lecture at the University of Havana on March 18, 1960, this is a historically orientated study of the *Revista de Avance*.

MENTON, SEYMOUR. "The Short Story of the Cuban Revolution." *Studies in Short Fiction* 8, no. 1 (Winter, 1971): 32–43. A concise review of the importance of the novel and short story in Cuba in the nineteenth and twentieth centuries along with commentary on trends in Spanish-American prose fiction of this century. Twelve anthologies of short stories published between 1961 and 1969 are singled out for special attention.

PEAVLER, TERRY J. "Prose Fiction Criticism and Theory in Cuban Journals: An Annotated Bibliography." *Cuban Studies/Estudios cubanos* 7, no. 1 (January, 1977): 58–118. This valuable research tool is an index of materials published in Cuba since 1959. Although there are only two listings that concern Novás Calvo, researchers can facilitate their work by consulting this study.

PORTUONDO, JOSE ANTONÍO. "Four Cuban Novelists." *Books Abroad* 18, no. 2 (Spring, 1944): 235–38. Points out that Novás Calvo is the most universal writer of fiction in Cuba and devotes attention to language, time, and the sense of magical fatality in his stories.

RIPOLL, CARLOS. " 'La Revista de Avance' (1927–30) vocero de vanguardismo y pórtico de revolución." *Revista Iberoamericana* 30, no. 58 (julio-diciembre, 1964): 261–82. A general survey of the contents and an evaluation of the artistic and intellectual significance of the *Revista de Avance*.

RODRIGUEZ FEO, J. "Los cuentos cubanos de Lino Novás Calvo." *Orígenes* (invierno, 1946): pp. 25–30. A skillful but gloomy article that laments the lack of a cultural tradition in Cuba and complains of the excessive pessimism of Novás Calvo's works.

RODRIGUEZ-LUIS, JULIO. "Lino Novás Calvo y la historia de Cuba." *Symposium* 29, no. 4 (Winter, 1975): 281–93. An examination of the presence of Cuban history in the stories of Novás Calvo which concentrates on "La noche de Ramón Yendía," " 'Aliados' y 'Alemanes,' " and "Mi tío Antón Luna."

ROMEU, RAQUEL. "Lo negro cubano y Lino Novás Calvo." *Symposium* 30, no. 3 (Fall, 1975): 266–77. A survey of the role of the black in Cuban letters and Novás Calvo's writings. The article contains one minor oversight—the assumption that *El negrero* was written in 1935 and originally published in 1940, rather than in 1932 and 1933, respectively.

SOUZA, RAYMOND D. "The Early Stories of Lino Novás Calvo (1929–32): Genesis and Aftermath." *Kentucky Romance Quarterly*, 26, no. 2 (1979). A study of six stories published prior to 1932 and "La luna de los ñáñigos" of that year.

———. "La imaginación y la magia en la narrativa cubana (1932–33)." *Caribe*, 2, no. 2 (Otoño, 1977): 87–96. Concentrates on the significance of the 1932–1933 period in Cuban prose fiction and studies Alejo Carpentier's *¡Écue-Yamba-Ó!*, Enrique Labrador Ruiz's *El laberinto de sí mismo*, and Novás Calvo's "La luna de los ñáñigos."

———. "Lino Novás Calvo and the 'Revista de Avance'." *Journal of Inter-American Studies* 10, no. 2 (April, 1968): 232–43. An examination of the importance of the *Revista de Avance* in Cuban intellectual life during the 1920s and of the evolution of Novás Calvo's writings (particularly his poetry) in that journal.

———. "On Lino Novás Calvo and his 'Maneras de Contar.'" *The International Fiction Review* 2, no. 1 (January, 1975): 67–68. Examines the importance of *Maneras de contar* in the evolution of Novás Calvo's narrative art.

———. "Time and Terror in the Stories of Lino Novás Calvo." *Symposium* 29, no. 4 (Winter, 1975): 294–99. A study of the motif of terror in the stories of Novás Calvo and the relation of this concern to time.

———. "Two 'Lost' Stories of Lino Novás Calvo." *Romance Notes* 9, no. 1 (Autumn, 1967): 49–52. An introduction and analysis of "La cabeza pensante" and "Un encuentro singular," two stories which had been overlooked by critics and forgotten by their author.

Index

Anderson, Sherwood, 19, 27–29
Anderson–Imbert, Enrique, 30, 121
Arenas, Reynaldo, 52–53
Asturias, Miguel Angel, 96

Balzac, Honoré de, 53
binary modes, 63–64, 66, 73, 92, 93, 121
Blanco y Fernández de Trava, Pedro, 45–46
Bohemia, 94, 96, 103
Bohemia Libre, 96, 97, 98, 99, 101
Bueno, Salvador, 94

Cabrera Infante, Guillermo, 90
Carpentier, Alejo, 45–46, 52–53, 118
Casal, Julián del, 57
Castro, Fidel, 96
Chacón y Calvo, José María, 59
chase. See pursued hero and ritual hunt
cinematographic technique, 55–56, 82
Cirlot, J. E., 100
Conrad, Joseph, 16
Cristóbal Colón (ship), 29
Cuban novel, 45–46, 52–53

decadence, 57, 74, 79
detective novel, 94
Diario de Madrid, 53
disorientation, 22, 26, 83, 116, 119–20
Durland, Addison, 22

¡*Écue-Yamba-Ó!* (Carpentier), 45–46
existentialism, 65, 118

fantasy, 37–39, 49–50, 71, 99, 100–101, 112–13, 115
Faulkner, William, 53, 80, 118
fear. See terror

Fernández de Castro, José A., 22, 29, 110
Fornet, Ambrosio, 25, 64, 80
fragmentation of form, 46
Frazer, Sir James, 45

Gaceta Literaria, 21, 25, 30
García Lorca, Federico, 58
Golden Bough, The, (Frazer), 45
Gorky, Maxim, 16
Gutiérrez, Gustavo, 22

Hays, Hoffman R., 64
Hemingway, Ernest, 10, 94
Hernández Catá prize, 64, 67
Hugues, Victor, 52
Huxley, Aldous, 53

Ichaso, Francisco, 16
Iduarte, Andrés, 64
imagery: geometric, 38, 41, 70, 87–89, 109, 119, 120; moon, 32, 35, 36, 44, 100, 111; spider, 41, 88, 100–101
irony, 24, 67, 75, 89, 121
Istrai, Panait, 16

Joyce, James, 29

Kangaroo (Lawrence), 53

El laberinto de sí mismo (Labrador Ruiz), 45–46
Labrador Ruiz, Enrique, 45–46
language, 26, 79–80
Lawrence, D. H., 53
Lévi-Strauss, Claude, 72
Lezama Lima, José, 92
Life, 94

Index

Machado, Geraldo, 65, 92
Martí, José, 102
Menton, Seymour, 99
Mier, Fray Servando Teresa de, 52
El mundo alucinante (Arenas), 52–53
El Mundo Gráfico, 53

narration, 22, 24, 26, 33, 39, 43, 78, 90–91, 92, 93, 104, 108, 113, 115, 116–17, *119–21*
Nenclares, Carmona, 58, 59, 101, 118
"Neurosis" (Casal), 57
Novás, Himilce, 60
Novás Calvo, Lino: appraisal, 64, 73–74, 80, 118–22; autobiographical elements, 75–78, 121–22; Cuban Revolution, 95, 96, *97–118;* early years, 15–16; relationship to the *Revista de Avance*, 16–20; return to Spain, 29–30, 53; Spanish Civil War, *58–59*, 60, 101–102

WORKS: DRAMA:
"El ahogao," 19

WORKS: POETRY:
"El camarada," 18
"Miedo," 18
"Proletario," 18
"Soneto a Federico García Lorca," 58
"Yo," 28

WORKS: PROSE:
"La abuela reina y el sobrino Delfín," 98–99, 101
" 'Aliados' y 'Alemanes,' " 60–64
"Angusola y los cuchillos," 103–104
"Aquella noche salieron los muertos," 23, 25, 30, *39–44*, 45, 57, 60, 64, 82
"El bejuco," *22–27*, 31, 34, 35, 39, 43–44, 57
"Un buchito de café," 97, 101
"Un 'bum,' " 102–103
"La cabeza pensante," *20–21*, 25–26, 31
"En CopeyAbajo," 117–18
"En el cayo," 23, 25, 30, *35–39*, 43–44, 60, 64, 67, 82, 88, 120

Cayo Canas, 64, 66, 67, 81, 83, *84–91*, 95
"Cayo Canas," *87–89*, 109, 119
"El cuarto de morir," 92–93
"La cuota," 59, 129n26
"Un dedo encima," 64, *67–72*, 87–88, 118, 120, 122
"Un encuentro singular," *21–22*, 25–26, 31
"A ese lugar donde me llaman," 93–94
"El esposo invisible," 105–108
Un experimento en el Barrio Chino, *53–58*, 75, 79–80, 102
"Fernández al paredón," *97–98*, 101
"El flautista," 20, 26
"Hacia donde se acuesta el sol," *110*, 119
"El hombre-araña," 90, 98, *99–101*, 120
"Un hombre arruinado," *18–20*, 25–26
"Hombre malo," *72–74*, 109, 119, 120
"Long Island," 72, 74–75
"La luna nona," *79–80*, 81, 89
La luna nona y otros cuentos, 64–80, 83, 95
"La luna de los ñáñigos," 23, 25, *31–35*, 39, 43–44, 64, 67, 72, 119, 122
Maneras de contar, 101, *103–12*
"En la masía," 59, 129n26
"El milagro," 97, 101
"Nadie a quien matar," 103, *108–109*, 110, 120
El negrero, *45–53*, 57, 60–61, 72, 73, 75, 92, 119
"La noche de Ramón Yendía," 19–20, *64–67*, 72, 83–84, 87, 88, 92, 118
"La noche en que Juan Tumbó a Pedro," 102
"Con un nudo en el corazón," 97, 131n3
"Los Oquendo," 91–92
El otro cayo, 95
"El otro cayo," 95; *See also* "En el cayo"
"Peor que un infierno," *103–105*, 107, 108, 110
"La primera lección," *75–78*, 92
"Quemando gasolina," 73

"San José," 59, 129n26
"No le sé desil," 89, 95
No sé quién soy, 81, *82–84*, 88–89
"El secreto de Narciso Campana," 109–110
"Mi tío Antón Luna," 101, *110–12*, 119
"En los traspatios," 81–82
"¡Trínquenme ahí a ese hombre!," 90–91, 105, 113
"La vaca en la azotea," 20, 90, 101, *112–116*, 117, 119
"Vida y muerte de Pablo Triste," 19, 26
"La visión de Tamaría," 20, 66, 83, *84–87*, 119, 120

Old Man and the Sea, The (Hemingway), 94
O'Neill, Eugene, 29
Orbe, 29, 30, 53
Orígenes, 92
Ortega, Antonio, 96
Ortega y Gasset, José, 22
Ortiz Fernández, Fernando, 45, 60, 84

persecution, *See* ritual hunt
Les petits bourgeois (Balzac), 53
Piñera, Virgilio, 96
Point Counter Point (Huxley), 53
Portal, Herminia del, 60, 97, 126, 132
pursued hero, 22–25, 65–67, 141 (Leal)

Quevedo, Miguel Angel, 96

Revista de Avance, *16–17*, 25, 58
Revista de la Habana, 22, 25
Revista de Occidente, 22, 30–31, 64
ritual hunt, 34–35, 67–72
Roig de Leuchsenring, Emilio, 22
Romance, 60
Rulfo, Juan, 118

Sanctuary, (Faulkner), 53
El siglo de las luces (Carpentier), 52–53
slavery, 36, 40, 41, 43, *45–52*, 60–61, 75
Social, 19, 22, 25
El Sol, 53
Syracuse University, 97

Tallet, José, 22
terror, 18, 26, 32, 36–39, 69–72, 87, 89, *118–19*
time, 18–19, 37, 120
Tres tristes tigres (Cabrera Infante), 90

Ultra, 60
unreliable narrator, 90–91, 104–107, 113–15

Vanidades, 97, 132n11
La Voz, 53

Washington, George, 102
Winesburg, Ohio (Anderson), 27

El Yauco Café, 16